The Art of Coarse Sailing

The Art of Coarse Sailing

Michael Green

illustrated by

John Jensen

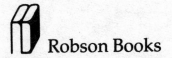
Robson Books

First published in 1962 by Hutchinson & Co
This revised edition published in 1995 by Robson Books Ltd,
Bolsover House, 5-6 Clipstone Street, London W1P 8LE

British Library Cataloguing in Publication Data
A catalogue record for this title is available from the British Library

ISBN 1 86105 002 X

Photoset in North Wales by
Derek Doyle & Associates, Mold, Clwyd
Printed by The Guernsey Press Company Ltd.,
Guernsey, Channel Islands

For
old friends

Introduction to the New Edition

Time goes by. When this book was originally written most yachts on the Broads were built of wood and didn't have engines and people used to arrive there by steam train. Now, not only is it difficult to find a yacht without an engine but the swines have demolished some of the railway bridges as well, so it's difficult to find a decent bridge to wreck your boat against. Most of the famous wooden-hulled boats of old, such as *Joan* and *Sabrina 1*, with their gaff rigs and natural cloth sails, have passed either into history or private ownership, and the quant pole is rarely seen. There seem to be about ten times as many motor-boats as there used to be, they are all five times as big, and going through Yarmouth or Horning in the summer makes one yearn for the comparative peace of the M6. And many of the old pubs have been transformed from little ale-houses into plastic hells. But then, that's true of sailing everywhere. And of life. It's all a bit more crowded and harsher.

People have changed, too. The characters in this book will seem rather old-fashioned with their constant harping on what they did, or did not do, in the war, and the way they smoke all the time. Not to mention the men's patronizing attitude to the women. Although sailing is a law unto itself. No sooner do some men get in charge of a yacht than they become raging lunatics. Crews of women sail round the world, girls cross the Atlantic, yet sailing still remains one of the great bastions of male chauvinism.

In revising the book for the new publication I debated

whether to bring it up-to-date but in the end decided against. To start with, things change so rapidly these days any alterations might be yet again out of date in a short time. In any case this isn't a textbook but the story of some sailing adventures many years ago, some on the Broads, others at sea, together with some advice on how to survive in the world of yachting.

And human nature doesn't alter. Somewhere, there will always be megalomaniacs skippering yachts, persecuted women in the galley, idiots in powerful motor-boats barging recklessly about the water, big boats bullying small boats, contrary winds and tides, surly professional watermen, bad weather, yachting know-alls, sailing snobs and sailing bores ... the list is endless. In fact I can't understand why I ever went sailing, except that looking back I got a lot of fun out of it, some of it the sort you get when you leave off banging your head against a wall.

So I've contented myself with a few cuts, a few changes and some additional material (one or two pieces of which came from the sequel, *The Art of Coarse Cruising*). I suppose Harry, Beaver and some of the other characters in the book might seem rather peculiar today but they represent the vanished race of true yachtsmen, scorning an engine, poling the boat through places where no yacht should ever go, always ready with an oath and a helping hand, and I am proud to have been one of them.

Finally, two warnings. First, don't dream of using this book as a pilot to the Broads, because they've changed a little in the thirty-odd years since it was written, and you may find one or two of the things described don't exist any more or have changed out of recognition. Apart from the fact that like most writers, I find it difficult to tell the truth.

Furthermore, ever since someone injured themselves trying to perform one of the strokes described in the companion book, *The Art of Coarse Golf*, I have been worried that something similar will happen again. I therefore do not take responsibility for any of the so-called advice given in this volume. The fact it worked for me does not mean it is infallible. I don't want angry widows writing and complaining, 'My darling husband would be alive today if he hadn't tied up the boat with the knot you recommended.' If you don't want to be widowed, invent your own knot. Or preferably, give up sailing.

Michael Green
London 1995

Foreword

The only reason I am writing a Foreword is because a friend said that the Foreword was the funniest part of *The Art of Coarse Rugby*. This rather hurt me, because I didn't write the Foreword to the original edition – it was written by Spike Hughes. So I'm taking no chances of a similar blunder this time.

My real purpose, however, is simply to thank everyone I have ever sailed with for so kindly – and unconsciously – providing material for a book. I should also include the strangers who have unwittingly helped, in particular the distraught honeymoon couple who had their first quarrel on the mud at Yarmouth. I should also like to thank Mrs Kay Eldridge for typing the manuscript. Considering that she nearly lost all her fingers trying to fend off my boat on one occasion, it was most kind of her.

1

Every year I swear I won't spend my holiday sailing again. Considering I say this annually, it's surprising how much sailing I've managed to do. Each time I return bruised, battered and suffering from incipient scurvy, with a great dent worn in my buttocks, and I say, 'That was terrific fun, but next year I'm going to do something restful.' And somehow twelve months later I'm banging the same dent in the same place with the edge of a cockpit coaming or crawling on hands and knees in some stinking bilge.

Not that much of my sailing has been particularly glamorous. I suppose most of it would qualify for the description Coarse Sailing. For those unfamiliar with Coarse sport I must refer to my definition of Coarse Rugby – a game played by fewer than fifteen a side, at least half of whom should be totally unfit. It is easier to define a Coarse Sailor than Coarse Sailing, and I think the following definition sums him up pretty well:

One who in a crisis forgets nautical language and shouts, 'For God's sake turn left.'

It's only your true-blue salt who can remember the *Manual of Seamanship* when charging into the side of a chain-ferry.

Here is an example of what I mean. I used to sail with an awfully knowledgeable chap who owned a two-berth sloop which he kept on the Hamble. Although he was most meticulous about using the correct terms ('I don't like the look of those baggy-wrinkles,' he used to say wisely), he wasn't much good really. He is the only man I

know who actually ran into the Isle of Wight while trying
to reach France.

One day I was at the helm and our course took us slap
into an oil tanker. As it was his boat, I asked him for
suggestions. All I wanted was something simple, like 'Oh,
go round the back of her.' Instead I received a stream of
the most appalling gibberish; things like 'Luff up and
leave her bearing Green-four-oh.' I asked his pardon
politely and he began to panic and ramble on about luffs
and bearings and baggy-wrinkles and lord knows what.
When a collision was nearly inevitable I shoved my face
against his and asked bluntly whether he meant left or
right. He never forgave me.

The trouble with people like that, and they abound in
sailing, is that they love making simple things complicated. Your Coarse Sailor likes to make complicated things
simple. And I write as one who has navigated across the
Zuyder Zee by means of two nails. We chartered the boat
up some Dutch canal a hundred miles from the sea and as
it had never occurred to us that you could get out of sight
of land in the middle of Holland we had no compass.
Unfortunately, we had forgotten about the Zuyder Zee,
which before they filled a lot of it in was as wide as parts of
the English Channel, and there we were in the middle
with the last landmark long since vanished.

The railway ferry from Staveren refused to slow down
so we could follow him and we rejected an idea by the
boat's lunatic that we should follow the gulls ('They
always fly towards land old chap'). Just when it seemed
we might be sailing round and round for ever, like some
modern Flying Dutchman, inspiration smote me with
almost physical force. I stuck a nail in the deck and put in
another at the end of its shadow. All we had to do was to
keep the shadow constant and we were bound to sail
straight.

Actually, by using this method, you follow the sun in a

vast circle, but it's all right over short distances. And if the story produces a howl of rage from some saloon bar Admiral I can only say that Columbus discovered America with not much more apparatus. Admittedly, he thought he'd found India, but this merely qualifies him as one of the first Coarse Sailors.

The true home of all Coarse Sailors is the Norfolk Broads. By Broads in this connection I really mean the system of narrow rivers that links the Broads proper, which are, of course, shallow lakes of differing sizes, delightfully pretty but dull from a Coarse Sailing point of view, since they offer few hazards apart from going aground for twelve hours.

It is fashionable among some yachtsmen who have never sailed the Broads to sneer at them and refer to sailing there as ditch-crawling. It is, indeed, true that if sailing is mucking around in boats then Coarse Sailing is boating around in muck, but the Broads do require special skills of their own.

I am thinking of problems like tacking a 28 ft boat up a river or dyke not much wider than the length of the boat. The banks are lined with anglers and approaching at high speed are three large motor-cruisers driven by people who think yachts have got brakes. That is a situation not unknown on the River Ant, although it's even worse sailing up the Ant with the wind astern, since you may well be trapped by boats behind while more bear down in front of you, so any chance of turning into wind is out of the question. The solutions to this sort of problem range from taking off sail in five seconds to leaping into the reeds with a rope and making fast to a tree. After that sort of ghastly experience whistling across Chichester Harbour with the wind on the beam is child's play.

That's the beauty of the Broads. They compress an awful lot into a short time. After all, Nelson learned to sail there as a boy.

There are other hazards which do not affect the salt-water sailor, and I speak as one who has put his boom through the window of a grocer's shop and caught his gaff on an electricity cable. You don't have *those* hazards in the Channel.

The Broads have certainly provided me with as much excitement as I or my friends have found sailing elsewhere. Over the years our small flotilla has suffered every known marine disaster. These include not only the more common upsets, such as going aground, being rammed, falling overboard and so forth, but others more exotic, such as Insanity of Ship's Master, Sinking, Death of Passenger, Burial at Sea, Restraint by Forces of Law and Explosion of Vessel, most of which are described in the following chapters. We have even been under fire on the Broads, when some fool let off a duck-gun as we passed along the River Bure and the pellets thudded into the mainsail. The ducks remained quite undisturbed while we dived for shelter. Later the lunatic who fired said he mistook us for a rare bird in the dusk.

The point about incidents like this is that they satisfy the inner craving of every Englishman worth his salt to feel himself a sailor, an ocean adventurer, a real member of the race which settled half the globe. It's that which makes people sail whether on the sea, the Broads or the Thames. That is why they put up with the appalling discomforts of sailing when they might be doing something more sensible, such as going on a cricket tour.

I personally cherish a belief that somewhere in the family was an old sea-dog. I feel sure that on the West Country side of our family was once a Brixham skipper named Jem Green. Jem was tough but lovable, the sort of skipper who was always writing things like this in the log:

March 1: Weather v. stormy. Water v. low. Crew v. mutinous. Food bad. Two hands dead of French disease.

March 2: Weather worse. French disease rampant. Hanged two hands. MEM: Sextant is faulty, or am sailing up Ludgate Hill.

March 3: Accidentally shot albatross in morning. Hurricane immediately blew up.

One also likes to feel that old Jem was a bit of a moralist in the best Victorian tradition, and the author of a poem running something on these lines:

Jem Green's Ode

> When the gale-force winds of adversity
> Cause a sailor to take in a reef,
> Then he ties the cringle of living clean
> To the boom of an honest belief.
>
> For you cannot luff through life, my boy,
> When the wind of ill-fortune blows.
> So make firm your grip on the tiller of hope
> And Heavenwards swing your bows.
>
> Then perchance it will softly come oe'r you
> That the main is awaiting ahead.
> And life will abound in its glory
> When the green on the starboard shows red.*

There is a great deal of old Jem Green in all of us, or so we like to think.

As there was in the little man I met in Bosham harbour, sitting smoking in a clinker-built dinghy and writing in a notebook.

It turned out that he was keeping a log of his holiday.

---

* Whatever that means.

Three days previously he had hired the dinghy from Itchenor, about two miles away, and had sailed round the corner to Bosham. Since then, he explained, the wind had been too strong to set forth again.

He showed me his log. It went something like this:

August 3: Sailed 09.00 hours. Wind force 2. Bosham 10.30 hours. Reported to Harbour Master. Returned to find vessel hanging from harbour wall owing to tide fall.

The next two days contained accounts of his peering out to sea and wetting his finger and deciding not to sail. He'd told me he was having the time of his life and he wished he's taken up sailing earlier. And I, for one, am not sneering at him.

This inner craving to emulate our adventurous forebears is not, of course, confined to Englishmen. At Einkausen in Holland I met a German who quite obviously dreamed of himself as Wolfgang von Jem Green. He had sailed from Hamburg, and as he told us he was an army officer we promptly nicknamed him General Rommel.

After examining our boat with a contemptuous air he suddenly said, 'Did you sail from England?'

'No,' we replied. 'We hired the boat over here.'

'Perhaps you have fear of the veend?' he suggested. 'My colonel he was coming with me, but he have fear of the veends. And my wife, she have fear. Everyone have fear. I do not have fear. I sail to England tomorrow.'

There was a roll of thunder in the distance. His eyes gleamed.

'Ah, it is good,' he said. 'We have a storm. Tomorrow plenty veend. I go sail to Hastings. You know Hastings, yes?'

He set sail early next morning in a storm of Wagnerian dimensions, with the lightning playing about him. The sequel, however, was rather disappointing. Two days later we sailed past him in Amsterdam harbour, where he was obviously moored for some time, since all his underwear was hanging out to dry. He pretended not to see us.

But the year the events described in this book took place I really thought I had escaped sailing. Everything was arranged for a peaceful trip to Budleigh Salterton when Beaver rang up and asked if I would like to come round to his house for a drink that evening.

Beaver is an old sailing friend, a fat, bearded bachelor of fifty who has nearly cost me my life on many an occasion. He may have a proper name but if so I've never heard it used. I'm quite sure if he were married the vicar would have to say, 'Do you, Beaver, take this woman ...'

When I arrived there was a group of people lying all over the front room examining charts and pretending they understood them. Beaver was having a pre-sailing conference. At these he outlines a preposterous route for the week which would be difficult for a hydroplane to complete, let alone a couple of old sloops. They were all old sailing friends, with one exception: a nervy, not unattractive girl of nineteen, who was introduced to me as Joan. She was the only person who had not sailed before and was bouncing around and asking questions like 'Do we have to sit up all night keeping watch or hosing the scuppers?' I told her that the only times when we sat up all night were to drink or when Beaver ran us aground.

'I think it's going to be *fun*,' she squeaked (I was to discover she had a habit of talking like something out of a schoolgirls' annual). Personally, I doubted it, for she was sailing with Dennis and Arthur, two of the most selfish bachelors that ever took a girl sailing so she could peel the spuds. Dennis – a precise, clipped sort of chap, who had been a naval officer in the war and couldn't quite forget it – had already handed Joan a typewritten daily menu which would not have disgraced a first-class hotel. Arthur was talking incessantly in a strange bucolic accent.

… outlines a preposterous route for the week

Nobody knows where he picked it up. He claims it to be a piece of genuine Fen dialect, but it sounds like something left over from the local amateur dramatic society. However, as he is a seed salesman, it sometimes comes in useful with the customers.

Beaver's tame slaves on this trip were to be Harry, who when sailing drinks a bottle of Worthington every morning as soon as he gets up, and his wife Sheila, who spends her time tending their ever-growing brood. After about six gins I became aware that Harry, Sheila and Beaver were treating me as one of the crew, saying things like 'We shall have to have steak this year, specially for Mike,' the cunning swines. I explained feebly that I was going to Budleigh Salterton, and Beaver said, 'Yes, of course,' and poured me two more gins. By the time he opened a new bottle I actually *wanted* to go on the trip.

Beaver produced a catalogue and showed me the yacht, *Merryweather II*, a worn-out twenty-eight-foot sloop described as 'ideal for the yachtsman with some practical experience'. This is the middle category on the Broads. The lowest is 'suitable for both novice and experienced yachtsman'.

The catalogue sang the praises of *Merryweather* in lyrical language. 'Roomy saloon,' it warbled, 'with easy-to-raise cabin-top. Extra berth in forepeak. Wash-basin. Toilet entirely separate. An extremely comfortable boat. Self-acting jib available.'

Translated into plain words this meant that the cabin-top would lift only under the combined efforts of three strong men, and was liable to collapse on our heads while we were having dinner. It would also slide overboard if we did a violent gybe. The wash-basin was just big enough to wash a finger in. The berth in the forepeak was designed for someone shaped like a letter S. When the cabin roof was lowered the toilet could be used only by a contortionist. The self-acting jib had never in all our experience failed to catch as it swung across, and far from saving labour usually required one extra hand whose sole duty was to kick it over every time.

Twenty-odd years ago Beaver used to secure the best and fastest yachts on the Broads, but after a series of disasters he found it increasingly difficult to do so. He tried changing from boatyard to boatyard but his reputation followed him and he finally had to settle for Loudwater's. While it would not be true to say that Mr Loudwater looked forward to Beaver's annual visits, at least he put up with them, and there was always the consolation that the damage he caused was so extensive it kept his men occupied during the winter when work was short.

Beaver's choice of boats was further restricted because he wouldn't go on one named after a woman, as many are. This was the result of an unhappy experience in his youth, when he owned a small sloop on the Solent. He went out with a girl called June so he called his boat *Beauty of June* (anyone who invents a daft name like that is asking for trouble anyway). June (the girl) had a few trips and on the second she met one of Beaver's men friends. To cut a long story short, the inevitable happened and June left Beaver for his friend Jim. Worst of all, Beaver is to this day convinced the affair was first consummated on board while the boat was lying at Lymington and he was ashore getting a loaf of bread.

'I knew something was going on as soon as the boat came in sight,' he said bitterly afterwards. 'It was a perfectly calm day yet the mast was swaying all over the place.'

After this he grew to hate the boat and used to bellow 'Faithless bitch!' at it if anything went wrong. Sometimes he even kicked it. He seriously considered changing the name to *Whore of the Solent*. Then he met a girl called Anne and promptly changed the name to *Anne*, and then one day I met him painting out the name again and I knew what had happened. So never call a boat after a woman (or a man, come to that).

We broke up at midnight and next day I wrote to the guesthouse at Budleigh Salterton:

My dear Mrs Jones,

I am sure you will be sorry to hear I shall be unable to spend the week of July 15 with you as planned. Yesterday I received news that my guardian has been taken ill in the Shetlands and is expected to pass away some time in the week beginning July 15.

It is indeed a tragic coincidence that this should happen as last summer you may remember I was called to Co. Cork, again to a sick relative's bedside.

Last year you may recall that in view of the unfortunate circumstances you were kind enough to refund my deposit on re-letting the room, and I wonder if you could see your way to do the same this time. Perhaps when you reply you could enclose the camera I left behind two years ago and about which I have written several times ...

2

According to Beaver's military-type schedule I had to report to his home at six-thirty on the first morning of the trip. Much to my surprise I actually arrived by ten to seven. After I had rung the bell for ten minutes his aged aunt appeared and told me her nephew was still sleeping. At that moment a window was flung open upstairs and Beaver stuck out his head and demanded what all the damn noise was about. I told him and he grunted and shut the window violently. His aunt vanished (she was that sort of woman, she had a knack of becoming invisible at a moment's notice) and I spent my time mooning about the front room looking at photographs of Beaver as a repulsive child.

It was half an hour before Beaver appeared, looking like a walking ships' chandlery, festooned in coils of rope and tottering under the weight of an incredible collection of marine junk ranging from binoculars to a hatchet.

'No breakfast,' he announced firmly. 'I'll get something at Newmarket. We've got to push on.'

Harry and his wife were on their fifth cup of coffee when we arrived. Sheila was looking rather depressed because their children were at her mother-in-law's. Far from depressing Harry, the loss seemed only to uplift him. 'Of all the sounds heard by the human ear, the vilest is "Daddy",' he said firmly while we waited for Sheila.

It took half an hour to load their luggage. That was Sheila's influence. You find that where a man will go sailing cheerfully for a week with just a spare pair of socks, women insist on taking such unnecessary luxuries as an extra corset and, of course, a dress ('in case we should go to a dance'). This gigantic mountain was somehow piled into the luggage rack on top of the car, and with a crash of gears Beaver drove off.

He drove to the end of the street at fifty miles an hour, braked violently at the corner, and the whole rack shot over the bonnet and nearly hit a policeman directing traffic. Harry and I risked death to salvage the stuff, snatching suitcases from under the wheels of buses. The only casualty was a tube of shaving-cream belonging to Beaver, which was run over by a lorry and squirted all over the policeman's trousers. He didn't notice because his attention was taken up with Beaver, who was cursing and waving his fists at a queue of hooting cars behind him.

At nine o'clock we started off again. We were late and Beaver's speed was nightmarish. At least it would have been, but I couldn't see much of what transpired because all the luggage was now inside the car and my view was restricted to one side of a large suitcase nursed on my lap. From Beaver's comments, however, it was possible to judge we were making painful progress along a road filled with lunatics and car-driving ordure (a favourite term of Beaver's).

The estimated time of arrival at the boatyard had been ten-thirty. We got there just as the staff went for lunch. *Merryweather II* was clearly not ready to sail. She had not been cleaned and was without blankets and a gas cylinder. Beaver gazed at her in horror and then addressed the boatyard men as they sat munching their sandwiches. In Napoleonic style he begged for volunteers to prepare the yacht as we had a long way to go before nightfall and was rewarded with some encouraging smiles and nods and jerks of the thumb in the direction of the yard office. Nobody moved, however. Harry suggested having a bite to eat but Beaver reacted as if someone had proposed a vote of thanks to the Pope at a Communist Party meeting.

'Sheila – get the stores from the shop,' he barked. 'Mike, help her. Harry, help me check the rigging. We'll sail at fourteen hundred hours.' Although Beaver used the twenty-four-hour clock to show we were now under command, he would secretly have preferred to say 'four bells'. Unfortunately, he could never remember how many bells meant what. His little speech, however, was rewarded with a cheer from the boatmen, who had heard it all before.

On the way to the grocery store Sheila drew my attention to an old Ford at the side of the road. 'Should the back of the car be like that?' she asked.

The car in question had an odd gap between the body and the mudguards. Through this could be seen a female posterior clad in leopard-skin slacks. There was something familiar about it. And sure enough, as we watched, Joan stuck her head out of the window, waved madly, and cried, 'Isn't this *fun*?'

Dennis, whose car it was, tottered from the grocer's carrying a large carton full of wine-bottles.

'Had a bit of bother on the way down,' he explained. 'All that patent metal substitute I fixed round the body gave way suddenly, and old Joan nearly fell out through the back. I'm going to write to the *Autocar* about it. I mean to say, they claim it'll withstand a weight of two tons and Joan doesn't weigh a quarter of that.'

Sheila gave a squeak. 'Oh, look, Dennis, there's a cat in your car.'

'As a matter of fact, it's mine,' said Dennis. 'I couldn't get anyone to take it for the week so I decided to bring it with me.'

I asked him where he was going to keep a cat on a boat and he said airily that he would probably tie him to the mast on a lead.

'He can swim,' he added. 'I tested him for buoyancy before I left by throwing him in a bath of water and he swam round and round like anything.'

There are times when I'm not sure whether I really like Dennis.

Ten minutes later an extraordinary thing happened. We all found ourselves in the pub. I have noticed this phenomenon before, especially when sailing. I hop ashore for a loaf of bread or something quite innocent and an unseen force drags at my ankles and I find myself marching willy-nilly into the nearest boozer. Harry was already at the bar when we arrived, furtively downing a pint of bitter and peering out of the window to see if Beaver was coming. He had slipped away on the excuse of looking for Loudwater, the boatyard owner, leaving Beaver to grapple with the boat.

What with one thing and another it was closing time when we left. Beaver heard us coming – for some reason we were laughing all over the street – and he was doing a martyr's act, making great play of swabbing down the deck with a long-handled mop. He had already set sail (not a particularly safe thing to do in the dyke) and the boom was swinging ominously in the gusts of wind. I noticed he had exchanged our original quant pole – a long, forked piece of wood used for pushing off and for moving the boat in a calm – for a much larger one, resembling a young flagstaff.

'No time to store that grub,' he shouted. 'Sling it in the cabin and cast off. We're behind schedule already.'

I handed down the packets of food to Harry, who passed them to Sheila inside the cabin. After the first few had been passed Sheila called for Harry to help her and he disappeared below. Beaver ignored the hold-up.

'Cast off for'd,' he boomed impatiently. I shovelled the rest of the stores on to the deck hastily, dropping a jar of pickles into the water. Now I like pickles, so I knelt down to try to fish them out. Beaver paid no attention. 'Cast off aft,' he said firmly, lost in his own dream world. A piece of the bank gave way and my shoulder slipped under as I groped for the pickles under water. Beaver was staring at the top of the mast and nodding wisely to himself.

'We're off,' he shouted. 'Harry, take the jib sheets. Mike, stand by with the quant pole. Sheila, stow the rond anchor. Jump to it, everybody.' He sawed the tiller back and forth vigorously. 'She's not making much way. Pull in the port jib sheet, Harry, and, Mike, give her a poke with the quant.'

At this stage I felt obliged to explain something.

'Beaver,' I said, 'we are still tied to the bank.'

Beaver came back to earth and looked around in bewildered fashion.

'Tied to the bank? Why are we tied to the bank? We should be in midstream by now.'

Harry appeared in the cabin doorway.

'Sorry I wasn't much help in that little hoo-hah just now,' he explained, 'but Sheila was being sick.'

Beaver growled and made sympathetic noises.

'As a matter of fact,' went on Harry, 'she's not very well. In fact, you see ... Well, the truth of the matter is that she's going to have a baby.'

There was a momentary silence, broken only by a tiny feminine sound down below. Beaver's eyes widened.

'Going to have a baby? Good God, do you mean *now*?'

'Oh no, not immediately. In about seven months.'

Beaver's relief was perceptible, but he was not mollified.

'You ought to have told me you'd brought a stark raving preggers female on my boat. Preggers, by George. We've never had that happen on the Broads yet, not in all the years I've been coming here.'

'I'm sorry.'

'Well, it can't be helped now,' said Beaver magnanimously. 'You'd better tell her she's excused duty on the jib sheets until she's better.'

'So kind,' said Harry, not without a trace of malice, and went below to comfort Sheila.

An elderly female, one of the boat cleaners, appeared at my ear.

'Excuse me, my dear,' she said, 'but Oi couldn't 'elp overhearing what was said just now. If your friend's wife's 'aving 'er confinement she oughter come ashore, you know. A Broads boat ain't no place for a babby to be born in. Shall Oi phone for the doctor at Ranworth?'

'Do you mind, madam?' interrupted Beaver icily from the cockpit. 'We are about to sail.'

'But that little babby ...'

'There will be no babby, as you call it, for seven months. But *I* shall have one immediately unless I am allowed to set sail. Nobody seems to realize that we've got to make Yarmouth tonight. Now will someone please cast off fore and aft?'

Having abandoned the pickles as irretrievably lost, I untied the forward line, ran along the bank and cast off the stern as well.

'Right-ho,' shouted Beaver. 'This is it. Grab those jib sheets, Mike. Harry, come up here and stand by with the quant pole. Sheila, don't be sick anywhere except in the lavatory. Jump to it.'

We moved forward a few feet and stopped. An aged boatman from the yard had seized our stern rope and taken a turn round a post, and was now looking quizzically at our sails and shaking his head. Beaver nearly exploded with rage.

'Let that rope go, you old fool,' he hooted malevolently.

The old man replied by winding in the rope a little more so that Beaver was subjected to the indignity of travelling backwards with all sail set while he sawed the tiller futilely. Having secured us, the old man said: 'You ain't-a-going to sail in this 'ere wind without a double reef, are you? We 'ad one chap back 'ere this morning with a hole in his jib big enough to put your 'ead in.'

'Double reef?' Beaver laughed. 'Double reef? In this breeze? Why, the water's hardly popply.'

The waterman looked sagely up at the trees bending in the wind beyond the boatyard buildings.

'I don't know what Mr Loudwater'll say if we 'ave to come out tomorrow and put a new stick in 'er.'

The mention of Loudwater, his old enemy, put Beaver really on his mettle.

'That's quite all right, my man. Mr Loudwater knows me very well.' This was perfectly true, since Beaver had decimated his fleet over the years. 'I may take in a tuck at Thurne Mouth if I think fit. And now would you kindly let go of my stern rope as I have to be at Yarmouth before dark.'

At the mention of Yarmouth the old man shook his head and chuckled. 'Yarmouth, eh? You're a right 'un, you are. Well, don't say I didn't tell you. I don't know what Mr Loudwater would say if he knew. Off you go, then.' He untied the rope and gave the stern a kick. 'But I'm telling you – you'll never get anywhere like that. Not like that you won't.'

It's strange how one always seems to set out on a sailing trip to prognostications of woe from professional watermen. Instead of the gay cries of 'Good luck, good sailing' which one would expect, there is simply a chorus of groans together with rude remarks about the set of your sails. In fact it's fatal even to discuss a trip with watermen. You just mention casually in the pub that you're hopping round the headland and all stare at you and mutter about death with these dreaded neaps/springs/winter gales/ summer gales/or anything else you can think of. Not that you ever see them sailing. They seem to spend all their time digging up lugworms in the mud and swearing at visitors. For years I used to pay attention to an old chap in a blue jersey who sat in a pub in Salcombe telling everyone it was all death, etc., and it was only two years ago I discovered he was a lorry driver. He pretended to have a deep local knowledge of the weather, saying things like, 'Mark my words, when there's mist over Bolt Head you'll get rain before morning', and I know for a fact he got it all from the TV.

But, then, professionals are awkward in every walk of life. One would think they didn't *want* trade. There used to be an old boatbuilder in Sussex who had positively to be begged to build a yacht. One of my few wealthy friends once went down there one weekend and airily explained that he wanted a handy little sloop built for next season and he wasn't going to be too choosy about the price.

The old man continued planing a piece of wood.

'You can't just walk in 'ere and ask me to build you a boat like that,' he said. 'Oh dearie me, no. I've got to find out whether I'm going to like you first. I wouldn't have one of my boats sailed by someone I didn't.'

'Well, what the hell do you want me to *do*?' asked my friend, flabbergasted.

'Just you come on down here every so often and ask me again,' replied the old man, still planing. 'Then we'll see if I can build you a boat.'

Well, my friend kept on going down there nearly every weekend for six months, and then just as his patience was exhausted the old man said quietly one day: 'No, I shan't build you a boat. I'm too busy.' My friend says that it was only by a superhuman effort he refrained from pouring a pot of glue over the old chap's head.

My garage is like that. They will do anything except actually mend cars. If you take in the car and ask them to repair it they look at you as if you've blasphemed.

'Why not take it to Smith's, sir,' they say. 'They specialize in this sort of work. Or better still why not sell it? Of course we can't take it, but someone else might.'

If you insist they produce their trump card – 'We shall

... passed from the shelter of the boatyard sheds

have to get the welder in from Hanwell and he won't come for nothing. It's five pounds as soon as he puts his goggles on.'

The trouble is that the rest of us can never get away with that sort of blackmail. I only wish editors would say, 'We shall have to get Green from Hanwell. It's five pounds as soon as he unscrews his fountain pen, you know.' Instead,

I suspect they think I'll write anything for a couple of guineas, and they're probably right. (Although this was written more than thirty years ago, unfortunately it still applies.)

'Old goat,' muttered Beaver, as we ghosted quietly down the dyke. 'Telling me when to put in a reef!' At that moment we passed from the shelter of the boatyard sheds and screamed round into the main river to a crash of breaking crockery and a cry of 'What the hell?' from Harry, who stuck a worried head out of the cabin.

We were off.

Despite everything, the departure was comparatively peaceful for Beaver. The previous year he had been so impatient he had loaded someone else's stores on the boat and set sail with them. This was discovered after two hours, but Beaver refused to return, partly because the stranger's stores were much better than his own and included some nice wine. However, the indignant owner pursued him in one of Loudwater's launches and forced him to give up the luxuries.

It became clear within an hour we were not going to make Yarmouth. The wind was dead ahead and so violent and flukey that time after time we failed to come round at the end of a tack and were blown ignominiously into the trees by the river, whence Harry and I extricated us with the quant pole. There was nothing new in the situation for any of us. It is just one of the hazards of Broads ditch-crawling. But I couldn't help wishing Beaver had double-reefed.

Sheila recovered after a time and came up to make some tea. Beaver peered at her sideways in an odd fashion. He had a fear of women, whom he regarded as unnatural creatures, and to have a woman on board who was expecting a baby caused him the greatest distress. I think he regarded her as a female Jonah.

Cooking on *Merryweather II* was not easy. Like many

Broads boats, she had the stove in the locker under a seat in the well, and access was gained by lifting the seat. Just as the kettle was boiling we blew into a tree and during the confusion Beaver plunged his leg into the cooking locker and leapt four feet into the air as a jet of steam went up his trouser leg. After that tea was banned and we opened a few cans of beer instead.

That sort of thing is inseparable from cooking under way, especially if the food is stored in thwart lockers. The usual thing that happens is that Cook opens one of the leeside lockers while the vessel is on one tack, tries to grab everything before the boat comes about, and fails, so that as you heel over the other way a cascade of jam-jars, bean tins and detergent packets streams across the deck. I recall going aground for five hours because the helmsman put his foot in a pound of butter and fell flat on his back.

Not only that, but we couldn't use the butter. We did make a tentative try but one look at the helmsman's foot decided us against it.

As the food slithered about the boat I was reminded of a friend who went to Cherbourg with one of those selfish men who treat their crew as slaves. My pal did all the cooking, of course, and when the boat lurched in a squall on the way back a joint of meat shot out of the oven and into the lavatory bowl, which was opposite. After a short struggle with his conscience my pal put it back in the oven, marking the bit which had stayed uppermost with a skewer and reserving the unpleasant side for the skipper. 'Delicious!' cried the captain that evening. 'Tastes different from that English rubbish we get.'

It was almost dark when we reached Thurne Mouth, where the River Thurne joins the Bure. Normally Yarmouth would be at least five hours' sailing away. Harry pointed this out to Beaver, who showed no sign of having heard and merely asked him to haul the jib sheet tighter. But just as we rounded the corner Sheila exclaimed, 'Look at that funny man over there!'

Through the gloom a dim figure could be discerned jumping up and down and waving his arms. And then it spoke, and the ghastly accent was unmistakable. It was Arthur.

'Boyur,' he boomed (Arthur always begins with a vague mooing sound when excited), 'why don't yew throw me a loin?'

'What's that about his loins?' asked Beaver. 'Is he in trouble of some sort?' We explained that Arthur wanted us to throw him a mooring-rope. Beaver looked even more puzzled.

'Mooring-rope?' he repeated. 'Why isn't he trying to make Yarmouth? He's not aground, is he?'

Arthur joined in from the bank, his voice indistinct in the rising gale.

'Boyur ... yew'll never make Yarmouth tonight ... too dark ... gale blowing up ... death ... destruction all round....'

Beaver pondered this for a moment and said suddenly, 'Tell him we'll make for Potter Heigham instead.'

Harry bellowed the reply as we turned violently. We never heard Arthur's comments because Beaver swung the boat round in a dizzy gybe and we found ourselves setting off up the River Thurne in what was now nearly a howling gale, but I saw *Quiet Dawn* being cast off as we sped round the bend.

It was almost pitch dark when we reached Potter, although fortunately the wind had slackened with the coming of darkness. Coming alongside and mooring should have been the work of a few moments. But not for dear old Beaver, who insisted that a simple rearrangement of all the boats moored by the bank would mean a clear space for us.

Within five minutes the river was a seething mass of craft. Those with no one aboard were cast loose and towed to new positions while Beaver in person visited all the other boats, explaining why he wanted them to move. He received one or two rude answers. By the time it was all over there was a gigantic trot of six boats moored abreast while *Merryweather II* reclined in solitary state by the bank. To make matters worse, people were returning from the pub and finding their boats had gone and creating a terrific noise, shining torches and crying out.

One or two people, not knowing their craft had been moved, boarded the wrong boats. I sympathized with their predicament, for I once got on the wrong yacht in Oulton Broad. It was a sister-yacht to my own and I had actually crawled into the forepeak to fetch something before I discovered my mistake. I was just about to leave when the boat rocked as two people came aboard and then I heard a man's voice say, 'It's all right, darling, there's no one here.'

I remained frozen with embarrassment.

A woman then said. 'Are you sure it's safe, Adrian?'

'Of course,' came the reply, a little too heartily, I felt. 'No one will find us here.'

'Oh, Adrian, I can't help thinking this is wrong. It seems so mean. What about Charles?'

'What about him? From what you've told me he ...'

At this point I could stand it no longer and coughed loudly. There was a moment's silence and then the woman began to scream: 'I knew it, I knew it. Charles is on board. He's waiting for us. He's got his old Service revolver with him. Oh, Adrian, why did we do it? Why, why, why?'

This geezer Adrian didn't exactly seem to be the heroic type because at the mention of the word 'revolver' he left the boat in two strides. The woman was not far behind. When I was certain they were out of sight I crept forth and scurried back to my own yacht.

Fortunately nothing like that happened this time, but

just when the confusion was at its height *Quiet Dawn* arrived with a shout of 'Boyur' from Arthur and came alongside the line of six boats which now resembled a small pontoon bridge across the river.

Beaver surveyed the chaos with satisfaction.

'It's much better when you organize things,' he said. 'Let's go and have a drink.'

SOME PEARLS FROM THE MUDBANKS

If the sun rises in the west, ring the coastguard at once.

It is never possible to make sure of fine weather in sailing, but to ensure rain and squalls, hang some washing out to dry on the backstay.

The human hand is a poor substitute for a fender.

Never put up an umbrella on a yacht; it suggests you may be a novice.

When grass and leaves appear on the bows, it is time to come about.

A tide is the best engine.

If during a storm a large bird perches on top of the mast, whatever you do, don't shoot it.

The finest way of surviving bad weather is to put three reefs in the mainsail; set the storm jib; prepare a sea anchor with an old canvas bag and a hundred-foot warp; make sure everything is securely stowed and the boat is well battened down; and then go ashore and sit in a bar until the weather gets better.

The only safe place for a spare outboard motor sparking-plug is the cutlery tray or inside the skipper's pyjamas. If placed with the engine tools it will disappear. This applies to all vital spares.

Never take advice from anybody you meet in a bar.

They will sneer at you for bringing your own tin-opener, until they lose the only one on the boat.

3

The last thing I remember hearing before going to sleep was an ominous howling of wind in the rigging and Beaver saying, 'Don't forget, six o'clock start tomorrow for Yarmouth.'

I was awakened by an insistent tapping on the shelf at the bottom of the bunk. It sounded as if someone were dropping a small pebble every few seconds. I heaved myself half upright and my thighs touched part of the bedding that was wet and cold. At the same time I became aware that it was raining cats and dogs outside and the wind was shrieking devilishly. It was pitch dark and the luminous alarm, set for the early start, showed three-twenty.

The cabin light revealed pools of water on the shelf, where a drip from the roof was tapping monotonously. There was a small pool of water on the side of my blankets. I was pleased to see there was also a pool on Beaver's blankets and a drip descending on the end of his beard as he lay on his back.

Up on the deck something seemed to have carried away. There was a slap-slapping of metal against the cabin roof. What with the gloom, the wind's howling, the splashing, and a soft snoring from Harry who was sleeping on the floor, the cabin was a dismal and eerie place.

When I swung my legs over the side of the bunk I trod on Harry's face. He emitted a stifled snort and bit my big toe. Beaver awoke, stared wildly about him and sat up crying, 'Cast her off … cast her off.' We never found out what he meant.

'It's all right,' I said soothingly. 'I think we've got a shackle swinging loose. I'm just going up on deck.'

'I'm all wet,' said Beaver plaintively.

'So am I,' said Harry, who was only semi-conscious. 'Who's been throwing water all over the cabin?'

'Damn stupid trick, that, throwing water all over the place,' mumbled Beaver, falling asleep at the end of the sentence and then waking up again. 'Ought to have more sense.'

I went on deck to be met by a blast of wind and rain which nearly knocked me overboard. I saw that the noise was being caused by the shackle on the end of the jib halyard which I had loosely tied round a shroud and which had worked loose in the gale. Knots are not my strong point. Ever since we found ourselves drifting through Yarmouth harbour at two o'clock in the morning Beaver has refused to let me make the boat fast and I must say I don't blame him.

Just as I retied the halyard, Beaver came up on deck. 'The cabin's leaking like a sieve,' he moaned. 'I bet old Loudwater's done it deliberately because he knew I'd be having the boat. I've half a mind to stop the cheque I paid him.'

We carefully examined the cabin-top. The water seemed to be possessed of supernatural power by which it could force itself through a solid roof. Not only that, but it kept leaking in different places, now sending down a small waterfall near the wall and then squirting a stream of rain in the centre. The whole contraption gave a fair imitation of a tea-strainer.

While we were looking round, the sound of voices came from the forepeak beneath our feet where Sheila was sleeping. Beaver was standing on the forepeak hatch and I was just about to suggest raising the hatch when it was opened from below by Harry.

I say opened, but he lifted it only about six inches at one

side. It was enough. Beaver tottered backwards, waving his arms and jerking his legs up and down as in a ghastly, nightmarish march, and vanished over the side.

He hit the water just as Harry put his head out of the hatch and said: 'Who's the idiot who's standing on the hatch? I couldn't get it open.'

Surprisingly, Beaver took the whole affair quite calmly. He was almost embarrassing in his determination to forgive and forget. Sheila, foolish girl, insisted upon giving up her bed for him, which was rather illogical because now the wettest person on the boat had the driest bed, while the driest (*ie* Sheila) had to have a wet bed. However, we arranged ourselves with Beaver in the forepeak, Harry on the floor and Sheila in Beaver's bunk. We had all settled down to troubled slumber when the boat rocked as someone came on deck, and Arthur opened the cabin door.

'Boyur,' he bawled, nearly cracking our eardrums. 'I just thought I'd warn yew that it's raining and blowing outside, so yew want to watch for leaks in that there cabin roof.'

We thanked him politely and said we hadn't noticed the rain but now he mentioned it there did seem to be a slight inclemency of the weather. Sarcasm is wasted on Arthur, however. Harry suggested Arthur might like to tell Beaver in the forepeak, in case he hadn't heard, and he clumped off happily to do so. I heard him lift the hatch and then there came the sound of it being suddenly closed and a shout as if someone had caught his fingers.

We saw no more of Arthur that night.

Dawn came after what seemed a damp eternity. Soon after six Beaver's alarm went off but Harry silenced it by throwing it out of the cabin and a rumbling from the forepeak showed its owner slept on undisturbed. That was more than we were doing, racked as we were by cramps through trying to curl up on the dry parts of the bedclothes. Sheila had got so wet she had climbed into bed with Harry on the floor. I must say it made me feel uncomfortable. It gave me rather a shock to turn and find her face about six inches from mine. For one ghastly moment I thought she had got into the wrong bunk and I would appear in the newspapers under a heading like

£5,000 DAMAGES AGAINST 'YACHT MONSTER'
'A Likely Tale' – Judge.

No wonder yachtsmen are always swapping wives and girl friends. After a week on a small boat you know more about a woman than her husband. I always remember one larky girl with a generous figure who used to mutter when you squeezed past her in the cabin, 'You've got to marry me now.' To which Harry always used to reply, 'I don't need to. I've seen it all, thanks very much.'

Actually, I'm a bit sensitive on this business of sleeping in the wrong bunk because of a terrible experience in the army when I visited a pal in another unit and stayed overnight in an empty bunk in his barrack-room. In the middle of the night three military police marched in and asked where Davis slept. A sleepy hand was waved at my bunk and the next thing I knew I was being dragged off to the cells, with the military police swearing I wouldn't escape this time.

Sheila brought me back to reality by complaining that she wanted to be sick.

Now this raised an awkward point. The lavatory was in the forepeak where Beaver lay asleep. Not to put too fine a point on it, the apparatus was a mere eighteen inches from his head. Before we could ask him to move, poor Sheila made an urgent effort to open the cabin doors, which promptly jammed, and then dived into the forepeak.

I don't think I have ever heard such language used to a woman before. Even Harry, who could not be accused of being the most attentive of husbands, was moved to protest, 'I say, Beaver, old boy, turn it up a bit.'

Eventually Beaver burst from the forepeak hatch, honking like a flock of wild geese and crying: 'My God, isn't it enough getting pushed overboard in the middle of the night without having some woman vomiting by my bunk in the morning. It's never happened to me all the years I've been sailing … never, never. Is this a boat or a maternity ward, that's what I want to know?'

There was nothing to do but ignore him, so we started to prepare breakfast. We were all on our hands and knees in the well, groping in puddles of water in the food lockers, when Arthur and Dennis arrived and demanded audience with Beaver, who was marching along the bank, sniffing the air and muttering, 'Preggers, by God!'

'Boyur,' said Arthur, by way of greeting. 'We presume yew aren't thinking o' setting sail today, at least not till this 'ere wind's gone down a bit?'

Beaver reared aggressively. 'Nonsense,' he said grimly. 'It's nothing. Just a morning blow, that's all.' A gust blew off Arthur's hat as he spoke. 'We're going to start as soon as we've finished breakfast. We'll never make Yarmouth at this rate. We're six hours behind schedule already.'

'Actually,' put in Dennis, in his precise way, 'it's at least Force Nine on the Beaufort Scale.' He produced a tattered yachting handbook. 'According to *Worthing's Yachting for Everyman*, this is defined as "Slight structural damage occurs (chimney-pots and slates blown off)".'

'Well, I can't see any chimney-pots being knocked off,' retorted Beaver. 'Does your book say anything about "Broads boats lay up wasting time at Potter Heigham all day"?'

'No, but it says something about skippers who set sail at their peril.'

'Nonsense. You'd better hurry up if you don't want to be left behind.'

'We'll let you know after breakfast.'

Our own breakfast was a miserable affair. Sheila

couldn't face frying food in her delicate condition, and Harry did most of the cooking. Harry is not the best of cooks. In fact, it would be no exaggeration to say he is probably the worst cook in Europe. His idea of frying an egg is to beat it with savage force against some hard object such as the deck and then to scrape up the remains with a knife and let them drip into the pan. He likes his bacon almost raw. I like mine well done. I got it almost raw. However, to compensate presumably, there was about half a pound of black fried filth mixed up with my egg, so I suppose I shouldn't complain.

Midway through the proceedings the Calor gas blew out and filled the boat with a nauseous stench. Beaver was terrified. He insisted the gas, being heavier than air, would sink into the bilge and explode later in the voyage. He recalled a night at Burnham-on-Crouch when a boat blew up and drifted blazing on to the other craft like one of Drake's fireships which dismayed the Armada off Calais.

The upshot of all this was that we had to get up the deck-boards and *bale* the gas out. I have rarely seen anything more absurd than two grown men solemnly baling nothing out of the bottom of a yacht and carefully tipping it over the side.

Two small boys on a motor-cruiser came and watched us and called out, 'Mummy, look at those funny men on that boat.' Beaver growled at them a good old nautical term for 'go away' and they repeated this to their mother in all innocence.

A man's voice – presumably that of their father – joined the conversation from the cruiser's cabin, saying loudly, 'Tell that man if he says that to you again I'll come over with a boathook.'

I rather admired Beaver's retort. 'It's all right,' he said, 'we've got a boathook, thanks.'

Fortunately, the outraged parent did not appear to hear.

After our apology for breakfast I walked to the famous

old bridge for a packet of cigarettes and passed Arthur's boat. It was an irritating sight. Inside the cabin Arthur and Dennis were sprawled in slippered ease, stroking the cat, while Joan, dirty, wet and with her hair all over her face, knelt over the stove like a slavey.

'Joan,' called Dennis from the cabin. 'There's no cherry on my grapefruit.' She left the egg she was cooking and hunted round in the well for a cherry. When she returned to the frying-pan the egg was looking rather leathery.

'Boyur,' called out Arthur. 'Yew know how I loikes my eggs, don't yew, me dear? I likes 'em crisp round the outside and underdone in the middle.'

Joan looked helplessly at the mess in front of her and then tipped the egg over the side and started afresh.

'Hurry up, me dear,' called Arthur, 'I've finished my grapefruit.'

Joan looked up bravely, determined to enjoy it all.

'I say, Mike,' she said, 'isn't this fun?'

Beaver and Harry were already untying the sails when I returned to *Merryweather II*. The wind howled dismally over the flat fields, and moaned in the telephone wires. Hardly anyone was about. A man in a yacht moored astern peered sleepily from under his awning and watched in a startled fashion as we prepared to set sail.

When all was ready Beaver marched down to *Quiet Dawn* and delivered an ultimatum.

'Are you sailing?' he demanded.

'I think we'll stay here and see how yew get on,' said Arthur, his mouth full of fried egg. 'If yew seem to be doing all right, then we'll follow on. Then if yew gets into trouble getting under way we can help yew, can't we?'

Dennis added: 'Have a cup of coffee. And by the way, Joan, there were some bits in the last lot. Can't stand coffee with bits in it.'

Joan rolled her eyes wildly.

Beaver refused coffee and we went back to *Merryweather*,

now swinging violently in the wind, which was gusting viciously. Harry looked troubled.

'It's blowing up, you know, Beaver,' he said. 'Don't you think we ought to wait?'

As he spoke a gull blew past, going backwards.

Beaver ignored the query. 'Just stand by to cast off, Mike,' he replied. 'Harry, get on the jib sheets. Sheila, keep out of the way.'

It is never particularly easy getting away from Potter Heigham. The river is only about sixty feet wide and there are boats moored each side. On this occasion the wind was dead ahead, and until we cast off we didn't realize how strong it was. A violent gust caught *Merryweather II*, the boat heeled over until the side-decking was under water and every food locker on the windward side fell open, so a cascade of eggs rolled across the well. Beaver trod on one and sat down suddenly. *Merryweather* shot across the narrow channel like a dart and smote a motor-cruiser moored on the opposite bank.

I have experienced many collisions on the Broads. They're inevitable on those crowded waterways. But I have never experienced one in which there was so much noise.

The shock of the collision knocked me flat on the cabin roof, where I had been standing, clinging to the mast. As I got up my ears were assailed by a deafening female squawking from the bowels of the cruiser.

Then a terrible Kensington accent said loudly, 'Are you all right, Mothah?' This was followed by more squawking and a clean-limbed young specimen of English manhood climbed up on deck, tying a silk scarf round his neck.

We sheered off and started to blow sideways down the river towards the bridge. I got one arm round the forestay and one leg on another boat to try to bring the head round, and found myself in danger of being split in half. Beaver was bawling a series of utterly incomprehensible and

… shot across the narrow channel like a dart

useless orders such as 'Back the jib … quant on the port side … tell that boat to get out of the way….' The boat in question had been moored for four days.

Young Kensington watched us in a bewildered fashion. 'Why don't you start your engine?' he called out.

Beaver appeared about to burst, but merely said some people preferred not to have them.

Harry saved the day by throwing the forward line to a cruiser skipper. I got the jib down without waiting for orders and we tied to the cruiser for a respite.

Beaver then asked, 'Why is that woman roaring with laughter?'

'She is not,' Harry told him. 'She is screaming hysterically in that cruiser in front. I don't think she appreciated being rammed by you.'

'I don't wonder,' shouted Beaver. 'Mooring in that stupid place. It was obvious someone would want to tack across there.'

A further outburst came from below. Mother was calling violently for Rodney. He disappeared, looking very worried. Sheila, who throughout everything had been crawling on the floor of the well trying to salvage food and was now scraping up detergent from a burst packet, started to take an interest.

'I really do think you ought to go and see if that poor woman's all right,' she said. 'She sounds frightful.'

'Of course the old cow's all right!' (Beaver talking.) 'What's she worrying about, anyway?' A thought occurred to him suddenly. 'She's not pregnant too, is she?'

Sheila ignored the crude remark. 'Well, I'm going to see how she is. And I think you ought to come too.'

'No, I won't.'

'Yes, you will. Harry, Mike, he ought to go, oughtn't he?'

'Yes.'

'Yes.'

'No.'

'Well, will you go if we all go?'

'All right, but you're wasting your time. We ought to be at Yarmouth by now.'

Mother turned out to be stout and middle-aged. She was reclining on a bunk with young Kensington tending her when we got aboard. As soon as our party entered the cabin she set up a piercing scream at the sight of Beaver and could be quieted only when he had left the cabin, after which he remained lurking outside, breathing heavily and muttering to himself.

Beaver had come aboard carrying a sheaf of accident reports which he requested the son to fill in. There was a slight hiatus when it came to the section *Whom do you consider responsible for the accident?*

Young Kensington simply wrote down the name of our boat so Beaver replied by firmly writing: *Act of God*. Later he was to receive a letter from the boatyard addressed to Mr God.

Mother would not be pacified. 'I knew we should never have come,' she wailed at Rodney. 'I told you we should have gone to Cromer.'

Beaver became tired of staying outside and pushed his great, ugly, bearded mug around the door.

'Madam,' he boomed. 'Where is your husband?'

This produced an unexpected effect. The woman voided herself of an immense screech and young Kensington seemed about to burst into tears.

'My father,' said Rodney bitterly, 'has gone off with Another Woman. I have taken Mothah on this cruise to recuperate.'

There seemed nothing more we could do. We silently slunk from the cabin, Beaver muttering, with what he no doubt meant as rough tenderness: 'I'm sorry about your husband, madam. I hope he comes back soon. But just remember there's plenty of pebbles on the beach.'

As soon as we were back on board *Merryweather*, Beaver was faced with mutiny. Harry stepped forward, clutching his forelock, and said, with a mock naval air, 'Beggin' yer pardon, yer honour, but the crew 'ave decided not to sail till the weather moderates.'

'Ha, ha,' replied Beaver. 'Jolly funny. Now if you'll just get the jib up we can head her round and ...'

We explained gently but firmly that we were not going to sail, and quanted *Merryweather* back across the river. Even that wasn't easy in the gale. Beaver immediately sat down with his tide tables to see if we could get away after lunch.

The crew of *Quiet Dawn* were sitting in the well, sipping cocktails and munching pickled cucumbers.

'Boyur,' called out Arthur. 'We saw your old spot of bother. I told Beaver he wouldn't sail out here today and I was right.'

'Joan,' said Dennis, 'there's no cherry in this cocktail. And put some more gin in while you're about things.'

Joan stuck her head out of the cabin door, her hands covered in potato peelings, and took Dennis's glass, giving me a look which had a touch of frenzy about it.

'I say, Mike!' she exclaimed. 'I watched you hit that cruiser. Isn't it all fun?'

The River Thurne flowed quietly on.

SOME USEFUL KNOTS

The Time Knot: Discovered by accident when I tied up the boat on a short line, and remembered three hours later that the tide fell six feet. On returning I found with relief that the knot had given sufficiently to allow the rope to pay out the right amount. The knot is tied as follows: Form a bight in the rope and slip it over the mooring-post. Then take the fall and make a loop round the standing part. Hold this loop in position with one hand and with the other hand pull the boat in a little to gather some slack and make another loop further down. Keeping the two loops in position, lift the original bight from the post with your teeth (or a third hand if you are so blessed) and pass it through the first loop. Carefully holding everything in position, walk slowly round the post four times. Place one foot against the rope to hold it in position (remembering

The Time Knot

all the time not to let go of your three loops) and walk round in the other direction. Then one by one drop the loops over the post. Pray.

The Granny Clove: A splendid knot for tying up someone else's boat (preferably someone you hate). Can be also used for holding up trousers. Pick up the fall of the mooring-rope and wind it twice round the post (be careful

The Granny Clove

not to wind it round your leg as well or the skipper may be faced with a choice between you and the boat). Flick the end of the fall over the standing part, whirl it round a bit, stand up casually wiping your hands and say firmly, 'OK,

The Mungle

Skipper, she's fast now.' It is best to stand on the rope until everyone is out of sight.

The Mungle: For tying up mutinous members of the crew. An old tea-clipper knot. Wind rope once round the waist of the offending seaman, pass one end to a colleague and both pull from opposite directions until the mutiny ceases.

4

At twelve o'clock we all went up to the pub, except Joan, who had to stay behind and watch over some exotic dish Dennis had ordered for lunch, and Sheila, who as a fellow-member of the Consolidated Women's Trade Union kindly offered to stay and help. Beaver arrived at the pub carrying an armful of charts and tide tables which he spread all over the bar.

'Now then,' he said, 'we shall have the tide against us after Acle Bridge so we can't waste any time. We've got to start as soon as possible – preferably after this beer.'

'Beaver,' said Dennis, 'look at those trees outside.' They were bending low as the wind whistled through them and at that moment a man opened the door and a violent gust blew all Beaver's charts on the floor.

'Boyur,' said Arthur. 'Yew can't sail in this. Look what happened this morning.'

'It was all the fault of that stupid old cow in the cruiser. Fancy mooring there! It was obvious we should have to tack out.'

'Perhaps,' said Harry, 'they moored there so as to be near the bank.'

This subtlety was lost on Beaver but we made the point. He agreed to wait until the wind moderated, provided he did not have to spend another night at Potter Heigham. When we were on our third pint the girls arrived, looking tousled and windswept. Joan was showing signs of mutiny. Asked what she wanted to drink, she replied hysterically, 'A double gin', and gave vent to a maniacal laugh.

'I hope,' said Dennis firmly, 'that you remembered to fry the meat until it was brown before putting it in the saucepan? And did you hang the bottle of wine over the side to cool?'

Joan's reply was to drain her gin-and-tonic in one gulp and giggle foolishly. I have seen the signs before in girls who go sailing. They start the holiday full of fun and pep, lured by advertisements which promise them a week of sunbathing on the cabin roof while the yacht heels to the exhilarating breeze. After the first day, when they are wet through, tired of cooking on their knees, raw with pulling on ropes, and probably feeling slightly sick, they change their minds.

Part of the trouble is caused by those fashion firms which advertise 'sailing' clothes, and display adverts of emaciated girls draped all over boats in some dress designer's idea of what to wear on the water. These clothes are usually fine for wearing ashore but have no connection at all with the true facts of yachting. The first essential of a girl's cruising outfit is that it should be proof against hot fat, boiling soup, etc. It needn't be waterproof because nobody cares whether the wretched girl stays under cover as long as she delivers the food three times a day. It should have large pockets for carrying knives, cigarettes, torches, matches, spikes and string, so these can be lent to male members of the crew who have forgotten their own and are blaming it on you. The outfit should also be designed so the wearer can put it on in a space four feet high and it should be big enough to fit male members of the crew who want to borrow parts of it. Instead of a jaunty yachting cap, the head-dress should consist of an electric torch strapped round the forehead, with a tin-opener strapped to the back of the neck.

We stayed in the bar too long and were all foolishly bold with drink when we came out. When Beaver said, 'Right, then it's agreed we have a quick lunch and sail immediately,' not a voice was raised in dissent, although we were standing by a newspaper placard which said:

60 MPH GALE HAVOC IN NORFOLK

The famous old bridge at Potter, near which we were moored, is very low and narrow. Yachts have to lower their masts to pass under, and even motor-cruisers have to drop superstructure such as hoods and windscreens. While we were eating lunch a cruiser tried to pass through the bridge at full speed, hit the arch and sent the entire cabin roof flying back over the stern.

How we all laughed! I have never seen Beaver so amused. I thought he would choke. There's nothing like seeing someone else in trouble when you're sailing to buck you up.

Our mirth was cut short when an aged human body was seen bobbing up and down in the water at the cruiser's stern, hopelessly tangled up in a rope. He had apparently been sitting on the stern and been swept off.

To say I am no hero would be an understatement. When duty calls and danger you will find old Green hovering in the background suggesting a compromise. But even I got as far as taking off my shoes before diving in when we were stopped by a shout from a local waterman who nipped into an outboard dinghy and pursued the cruiser, still heading full tilt upstream with the old man bobbing behind it while everyone on the cruiser's bridge was arguing whose fault it was.

They went a hundred yards like this before the waterman's shouts made them look back and they discovered father-in-law was no longer with them. Even then they didn't realize where he was and started looking all over the deck. When they did discover the woman driver gave a shriek of horror and drove into the bank, where the old chap was disentangled and hauled out. I did not, frankly, expect to see him alive, but he suddenly sat up, shook the water from his ears, and said loudly, 'When is the next train back to Nottingham?' I think he caught it, because half an hour later we saw him carrying his suitcase to a taxi.

Our lunch was a frugal meal of pork pies, but over in *Quiet Dawn* they had a big spread and asked us to sail first so that they could finish the wine. This time Beaver declined to risk sailing across the river and we quanted past the moored boats. The wind was really too strong even for that. As soon as one pulled the quant from the water at the stern the boat's head fell away and she blew sideways towards the bridge.

Quanting is one of the old Broads traditions that are dying out. Nowadays people just start the engine when they can't sail, or even when they can. But we have no engine and prefer the 'wooden topsail' as the old-timers call it, despite the constant drip of water down your sleeve and the danger of falling in or rupturing yourself when the quant sticks in the mud. There's solid satisfaction as you march along the deck with the quant pressed into your shoulder like a lover, and my only regret is that I've never quanted a Norfolk wherry, although I've seen it done, and an incredible sight it is to see one man moving thirty or forty tons with nothing more than a huge pole.

Indeed, I love quanting so much that at times I have been known to refer to the quant as 'my bride' and to speak ecstatically of my beloved, like a cricketer with a favourite bat. But today I got a large splinter in my hand ('Your darling bit you,' as Harry put it) and a crowd of ghoulish spectators gathered in their raincoats on the bridge scenting trouble and making fatuous remarks like 'Dad, why is that boat going sideways?' There was not another boat, powered or sail, under way. Everyone was battened down listening to the wind's scream and the pattering of rain on the canvas.

Arthur and Dennis had finished their wine when we

crawled past and were on to liqueurs and cheroots. All I saw of Joan was her backside sticking out of the cabin as she searched for Dennis's tobacco pouch, so I gave her a cheery hail and was rewarded by an unidentifiable noise in which one word sounded like 'fun'.

Normally I quite like quanting …

Arthur gave an ominously sly grin and called out, 'Boyur, we'll let yew get well clear before we start moving.'

Beaver planned to set sail at the end of the moored boats, where bungalows and trees provided some shelter from the wind and there is more room to manoeuvre. We had just started to hoist when an employee of a local boatyard, who had been watching from the other bank, shouted, 'You ain't going to sail in this, are yer?'

'Yes,' said Beaver.

'I forbid you to sail,' came the reply. 'You must be blamed mad. You come down 'ere of a holiday time, mucking about the river as if you was driving a crane....'

This stung Beaver.

'I commanded 300 men like you in the war,' he remarked haughtily. But the man was equal to the insult.

'Ah,' he said, 'and I shot 300 men like you in the war. And any of 'em could have handled a boat better'n you.'

The argument was cut short as Harry cast us off and dived inboard as *Merryweather II* swung round under the jib.

That first hair-raising charge across the river was rather emoting, as they say, but this time we had room to come about and make another tack. Beaver was at the helm, Sheila was on the jib sheets, Harry was lighting cigarettes for us all and I was in the bows coiling ropes and keeping an eye out for obstructions.

The first of these was a large, six-berth yacht, manned by four young lads, shooting upriver under bare poles and out of control. At first we thought it must have an engine, but as we passed one of the boys called out, 'How can we stop this thing?' They went out of sight round a bend and in the distance there was a cry of 'Boyur' and the sight of a mast waving madly. Most gratifying.

The next vessel was another yacht, also out of control, but this one *had* an engine. There was a man and a woman on board and they'd left the cabin awning up. The gusts of wind were too strong for the puny outboard engine with all that freeboard and they were breezing sideways along the centre of the river, wringing their hands (having an auxiliary engine does that to people, they just sit helpless when the wretched thing won't work). I had no doubt that we should see them later in the trip with the engine working at full speed and all sails set.

About a quarter of a mile downstream there was an eerie drop in the wind. The moaning in the trees died away and there was an utter silence. Beaver cut short his tack to avoid a fisherman driving a motorized dinghy down the centre of the river and *Merryweather* shivered uncomfortably as we came into wind. Next moment a huge gust tore across the water, whipping a little spiral from the surface, and as we paid off it hurled us towards a bungalow running down to the waterside. Beaver put the helm down but it was too late. *Merryweather* would not respond in time.

From my perch in the bows I had an excellent view of a perfect family picture as we headed for the bungalow's french windows. It was the sort of vision politicians paint of the average happy British home. It would have brought tears to the eyes of anyone who had seen it. There was Father, a baldish forty, smoking a pipe and reading the *News of the World*. Grandfather dozed in a corner. The wife was knitting, while a white-haired old granny was reading the other half of the *News of the World* (the bit with the dirty court cases) and tut-tutting to herself as she gloated over it. A delightful golden-haired girl of eight played on the carpet with a gurgling baby. The fire blazed cheerfully.

The scene changed in an instant as Mother looked up and saw a five-ton sloop, with a long, pointed bowsprit, hurtling towards the french windows. I heard nothing, but in mime saw the whole lot of them fixed in horror as *Merryweather* bore down.

I thought the bowsprit would go through the television set. Actually it didn't quite reach the windows, as it rode over the wooden piling at the end of the lawn and was stopped violently by the bobstay digging deep into the rotten wood.

Inside the bungalow, if pandemonium did not reign, it had a working majority. There was an impression of waving arms and legs and then five pairs of eyes were staring through the windows (the baby wasn't watching). On the boat all was order and calm. Everyone was lying flat on the deck and the yacht was fixed firmly by the bow.

I hopped ashore and made ingratiating noises at the family. Father was trying to open the doors, without much success, so I hoped to be able to hurry away before we became involved in any more trouble. I pushed against the bow but nothing happened. Finally I lay on my back and pushed the bow with my feet. Still nothing happened. The bobstay remained firmly wedged in the piling.

The doors opened at last and Father stepped forth, followed by his brood. The little golden-haired girl, I noticed, looked much less attractive now. She had an evil expression and was chanting, 'Wasn't it naughty, Mummy, wasn't it naughty of that man to do that?' The old grandfather was muttering something about 'them blamed schooners careering about the canal'. But Father was of a more forgiving disposition. He knew all about the river. Didn't he come down from Leicester every year to the waterside bungalow?

'Stop grizzling, Phoebe,' he commanded the infant. 'Can I give you a shove?' I asked him to put his hand firmly on the bow and push with all his might while I did the same. We pushed. Nothing happened. Father took off his coat, got his shoulder against the boat, leaned at a fearful angle and pushed even more heartily. This time he fell over.

'It's no good, Beaver,' I called. 'We're stuck. We're aground on this bungalow.'

'Nonsense.'

Beaver came ashore with Harry. We all pushed, and even Grandfather joined in, but all that happened was that Grandfather dropped his spectacles and for one agonizing moment they hung poised on the edge of the river before Harry rescued them. Following that the family retired, except for Father, who hung about making futile suggestions such as 'Why don't you unscrew that long stick poking out of the front?'

Just when it seemed we should be there for ever I remembered the collection of marine junk in Beaver's luggage, which included every tool known to man, and a few probably unknown.

'Why don't we saw the boat off,' I suggested.

Beaver glared angrily.

'You mean saw through the bowsprit?' he snarled. 'What a damn stupid suggestion.'

'No,' I replied, 'saw through the jetty.'

So in the end we did so. We sawed a large triangular piece out of the wooden piling and sailed away with it dangling from the bobstay. The family waved us a warm goodbye. We had made their holiday, even if we had nearly wrecked the bungalow.

Just as we were freed, Arthur, Dennis and Joan sailed past, jeering and waving so hard that they lost control and nearly rammed us. Joan was just visible as a pair of eyes over the cockpit coaming as she prepared hot toddies over the stove.

Beaver was furious. No sooner had the last sliver of wood parted than he commanded us to cast off and pursue 'that floating gin-palace'. The wind was as bad as ever and by the time we were well under way (after a couple of alarming false starts in which we nearly sailed into the bungalow again) the others had a good lead on us.

We lost sight of them and then caught up on a nasty stretch where the bungalows and trees end and the wind can scream unhindered round a bend. *Quiet Dawn* was in the reeds, rocking wildly, while Dennis poked about with the quant pole. The sight cheered us up no end.

Our companion boat was the only craft we saw on the river as we tacked down towards Thurne Mouth in a wind that was rising, if that were possible, and in scuds of rain. We went into the reeds three times, took the jib off and went in again. By the time Thurne Dyke was reached even Beaver had had enough and it was agreed to moor there for the night.

Thurne Dyke is a pretty little backwater off the mainstream, about 200 yards long. The scenery is typical: flat fields with black-and-white cattle grazing as far as the eye can see, windmills dotting the skyline and one particularly well-preserved mill by the dyke itself. When the fenland that formed the Broads was drained 300 years ago the earth shrank until most of the fields were below the level of the rivers, so the Broads windmills were built for pumping water to drain the fields. Although Thurne Mill stands by itself, many mills have a derelict steam pumping house next to them, and beside that a modern electric pumping station which has superseded the steam.

Normally, the fields appear to be full of white sails from the yachts on the rivers, but not on this occasion. *Merryweather II* and *Quiet Dawn* were alone.

The first time I sailed into Thurne Dyke, and that was some years previously, I went in at a spanking rate with the wind behind me, only to find that there wasn't room to turn round and come about into wind. We zoomed down the dyke, with the end looming nearer and nearer, our boom almost brushing moored boats, and no solution in sight. Then we remembered the mud-weight, a great block of metal which is the Broads equivalent of an anchor. It was a race against time to drag it from the forepeak and

make it fast astern before dropping it, when it pulled us up
all-standing. I have looked through the many books on
yachting to find advice on a situation like this and there is
none. They seem to concentrate on more esoteric
problems.

Beaver approached the dyke with unusual caution, took
sail down at the entrance and had the boat walked along
to a mooring. *Quiet Dawn* arrived half an hour later. We
had taken three hours to cover a stretch that would
normally take one. This fact had not eluded Beaver, who
spent the evening reshaping the schedule.

The last thing I remember before I dropped off to sleep
was the wind shrieking outside, the rain pattering on the
cabin roof and Beaver saying: 'Dawn start tomorrow.
We've got to make Yarmouth by lunch.'

A COARSE SAILOR'S BEAUFORT SCALE

SPECIFICATION OF BEAUFORT SCALE

Beaufort number	Description of wind	For Coarse use, based on observations made at Potter Heigham and Bosham	For use on land, based on observations made at land stations	Speed in nautical mph
0	Calm	Boat moves sideways with tide	Cigarette smoke gets in eyes	Less than 1
1	Light air	Coarse yachtsmen hoist sail, then wind instantly drops	Wet finger feels cold	1–3
2	Light breeze	Tea-towels blow off rigging	Public-houses close one window	4–6
3	Gentle breeze	Coarse boats career. Difficult to make tea under way	Public-houses close two windows	7–10
4	Moderate breeze	Gas keeps going out	Beer froth blows off	11–16
5	Fresh breeze	Coarse sailors get book on sailing from cabin and turn up bit on reefing	Customers in public-house gardens go inside bar	17–21
6	Strong breeze	Coarse sailors try to double reef and go aground	Elderly customers have difficulty in leaving public-house	22–27
7	Moderate gale	Coarse sailors rescued by launch	Public-house door cannot be opened against wind	28–33
8	Fresh gale	Aaaaaaaaah ...	Public-house sign blows down	34–40
9	Strong gale	Coarse sailors in public house	Coarse sailors struck by falling sign	41–47

NB – Although the Beaufort Scale goes up to Force 12 it is felt unlikely that anything over Force 9 would interest Coarse sailors except in a television programme.

5

Once more it was a disturbed night, this time due to Harry's snoring. It really was the most dreadful noise. My old car made a similar sound shortly before expiring on Ealing Common. That was rather an unusual experience because the car simply dissolved. All the parts wore out at the same time and it disintegrated, swerved across the road and hit a tree. The headlights, which had not worked for six months, blazed on and refused to go out. I remember the policeman asking me why I was wearing one trouser clip on the left leg while driving, and I explained that whenever the car went through a puddle a jet of water used to shoot up by the hand-brake, so I had to take this precaution. He thought I was trying to be funny.

Yachtsmen, who find snoring a menace in the confined quarters of a cabin, have several ways of trying to stop snoring and we tried them all. My own theory is to give the offender a short, sharp shock, for example by clapping your hands loudly in his ear. I did this for five minutes until someone in the next boat called out, 'I don't mind your friend snoring, but do you have to blasted well applaud him?' So we gave this up and tried Beaver's solution. He believes that one should whisper continually 'Stop snoring' in the ear of the offender. This message would eventually penetrate the subconscious, he said, and the snoring would cease. So he knelt by Harry, looking rather as if he were praying, and whispered gently at him. This had no effect and he gradually whispered louder and louder until eventually he was bellowing 'STOP SNORING!'

at the top of his voice. Harry woke up and asked what all
the noise was about.

Ten minutes later, when we had all settled down, he
was as bad as ever. I thought he would bring the mast
down. I was still convinced a sharp shock would do the
trick so I sprinkled a few drops of water on Harry's face.
The snoring rose to a climax and then he woke up.
This time we made him promise not to sleep until we were
all asleep. Twice he fell asleep first and we woke him up
and told him to wait, and then we all fell into deep
slumber.

During the night I had a dream about my ancestor Jem
Green. I was sinking in a storm-tossed ketch when Jem
appeared in a lifeboat, wearing an enormous set of
Victorian oilskins, and called on me to jump. I tried to
vault the boat's rail and couldn't. Lead weights were tied
to my feet. Just as the boat foundered, Jem gave a great
shout and I woke up. Then I became aware that the noise
was still going on.

It took a few moments to orientate myself. When fully
conscious I realized the noise was coming from Beaver,
who was sitting bolt upright in his bunk with his arms
outstretched and eyes tightly closed and shouting his
head off. He was calling out, 'Jump for it … Jump for it …'
and then lapsing into a burble. Finally he gave a great
shout, fell back on the bunk and slept like a babe.

The noise had awoken Arthur, who loves to spend the
night wandering abroad, and he arrived, clumping about
in heavy boots and thoroughly disturbing everyone. He
nodded sagely when we told him what had happened and
recalled that many years ago, when he and Beaver had
gone sailing, they had moored over a submerged stake
which went straight through the bottom of the boat as the
tide fell. They awoke in the middle of the night to find
water lapping all round. Beaver had made a gallant effort
to salvage something and was still in the cabin when the

boat gave its final lurch. He swam out clutching a toothbrush. Ever since he had been subject to nightmares while afloat.

The only person undisturbed by all the commotion was Beaver himself, whose heavy breathing showed that he, at least, was having a good night.

We awoke at seven-thirty to a glorious, sunny morning. The storm had blown itself out and for the first time I felt I was on holiday. I even got up first, it being my turn to make the early-morning tea. By an extraordinary coincidence Joan was also making tea on *Quiet Dawn*.

When I took Beaver his cup he demanded to know what all the row had been about in the middle of the night. He complained he had been awakened by me and Arthur arguing about something. Told he was the centre of the commotion, he refused to believe it.

'Nonsense,' he said. 'I was asleep all the time until you woke me up.'

He lowered his voice confidentially.

'Actually, old man, I reckon it was Sheila who disturbed you. These preggers women get strange fancies, y'know. I've been watching her closely. She's got that faraway look in her eyes. I wouldn't trust her on the helm like that.'

By nine o'clock we were on the move. It should have been an easy sail on a broad stretch of the River Bure but so many anglers were out it was like sailing up a tube. Anglers can never understand why a yacht has to zig-zag up the river and as for some reason they believe it is easier to move a five-ton yacht than haul in a two-ounce line, a clash is inevitable.

We were soon faced with a trial of wills, heading straight on the starboard tack for an angler who refused to draw in his line and just glowered at us. At the last moment he dragged in his line and shouted, 'Why can't you sail straight?' There wasn't time to tell him although behind us, Arthur, who does a little fishing himself, was in fact trying to defy the wind in an effort to avoid his fellow-anglers. The only result of his kindness was that he luffed and paid off straight into a sort of nest of anglers, who judging by the litter around them hadn't moved for a month.

Tact isn't Arthur's strong point and while the fishermen pranced up and down and abused him, he started handing out simple advice, things like, 'Actually old boy, you'll never catch anything here, you want to try ledgering with a bit of herring further downstream ...' When he sailed off, puffing at his pipe, I was surprised to see he was followed by a stream of anglers running along the bank, shaking their canvas stools in rage and hurling loaves of stale bread at the boat while Arthur nodded and hummed to himself. It took him five minutes to discover he had a complete rod and line wrapped round the front of the boat. When he did so, he was far too scared to land and threw the whole lot on to the bank and fled.

What with the anglers and the fact that it was the Broads morning rush-hour, things were rather difficult. The river was filled with six yachts tacking to and fro and something like a dozen motor-cruisers trying to get through in both directions. These included a mobile orchestra of guitar-playing youths who roared straight through the whole fleet at top speed sending two yachts into the bank and drenching half a dozen fishermen with their wash.

The cruisers seem to get bigger and bigger every year, and there are more and more of them. I can't think why they don't regulate the size and numbers. Since anyone without experience is entitled to hire a forty-foot boat and drive it down the river without reference to the rules of navigation, some of these boats can be a menace to cruisers and yachts alike.

Yachts, of course, are the most vulnerable craft especially when tacking. The ideal cruiser helmsman creeps up close and sneaks round the stern of the yacht as it comes about, or when signalled to do so. Unfortunately, a Broads yacht skipper frequently can't signal his intentions because what with the variable wind and the crowded river he doesn't know what they are. A new marine signal is needed: 'I do not know what is going to happen in this blasted wind', perhaps a question-mark hoisted in the shrouds.

However, I must not be unjust to cruisers. Whenever I am on one I never cease to be amazed at the calm sanity of the motor-boat crews and the lunacy of yacht helmsmen. It's just when I'm on the yacht all cruiser skippers seem to be blind and deaf. And every time I have been given a tow by a cruiser I have felt nothing but admiration for the consistent courtesy and navigational skill displayed. This feeling lasts at least five minutes.

Beaver handed over the tiller for a time and vanished below while I took over. When Beaver gives up the helm one never feels really in command. At times of crisis he is liable to seize it from your grasp and blame you for the subsequent collision. This time I was just congratulating myself I had the boat on my own for a few minutes when the hatch over the lavatory opened, and Beaver stuck his head out and shouted: 'Stop pinching her. Put your helm up a bit.'

Having discovered this novel position of command, Beaver was in high glee, and he spent a full half-hour sitting there distributing orders.

Talking of toilets reminds me of the time when I went on holiday in a boat so small it didn't have a toilet. There were two buckets, one with a red band and one with a blue band. The red bucket was the toilet, the blue bucket for washing up, etc. Or so I thought until the first evening when my companion swore it was the other way round and he'd been using the blue bucket for toilet purposes. As I'd just washed up in it, this was rather alarming. For the rest of the trip we dared not use either bucket.

At Acle Bridge, *Quiet Dawn*, which was ahead, stopped to take down the mast to pass under the bridge. To gain an advantage Beaver decided to shoot the bridge, *ie* take the mast down under way, glide through and raise the mast on the other side in midstream.

The mast on a Broads boat is pivoted with a heavy weight at the bottom. In theory it is easy enough to raise or lower, taking the strain on the forestay, but in practice the effect of the forestay is lost as the mast becomes nearly horizontal and you have to be careful the mast doesn't crash down.

All went suspiciously well at first. We took sail off and about a hundred yards from the bridge Harry grasped the forestay, and I kept both feet firmly planted on the counterweight at the bottom of the mast as an additional precaution against accidents while Beaver tugged gently at the mast to start it moving. It had just started to come down when a motor-cruiser passed us flat out and the wash knocked Harry off his feet. Beaver lost his balance as well, and instinctively clung to the mast for support, which merely pulled it down faster. The only things exerting force in the other direction were the weight at the bottom of the mast and me standing on it.

Sometime I should like an engineer to work out the exact forces to which I was subjected in terms of foot pounds per square inch as the mast came down. They would probably be sufficient to do something unlikely, such as lift two dozen eggs a distance of 300 feet. Anyway, they were powerful enough to hurl me upwards and outwards. I had a fleeting glimpse of Harry's startled face on the deck beneath and then I was four feet under the River Bure. I recall being surprised at how salty the water was, considering we were a dozen miles from the sea.

I have a horror of coming up underneath a boat so I swam lustily under water while my trousers ballooned about me with the air trapped inside before becoming soaked and pulling me down like lead weights. As usual on these occasions, I was swimming in the wrong direction and surfaced just by the stern. From what I could see, unhappy though my predicament was, I was well out of things by being overboard. The tiller swung unattended as Sheila, who had been on the helm, sat helpless in a cocoon of ropes and rigging (heaven knows why the mast didn't hit her on the head). Beaver lay apparently lifeless on the cabin-top. Harry was picking feebly at the wreckage.

As I hauled myself inboard, Beaver raised his head and said, 'Good God, what happened?'

A familiar voice called from the bank. 'Boyur,' came the rustic accents of Arthur, 'yew got that there mast down a bit quick, didn't yew?'

In fact, despite the chaos, we had achieved what we set out to do and were now drifting through the bridge in a haphazard fashion, watched by the inevitable crowd of ghouls. The simplest way of clearing the mess was to raise the mast again, but it had to be done quickly. One doesn't drift around sideways near Acle Bridge for long without someone hitting you.

Harry heaved on the forestay, while Beaver and I lifted from the cabin-top. The mast groaned up a few inches and then stuck as the shrouds caught the corners of the cabin. Beaver got them free, called for a mighty effort, and we all heaved. This time we were stopped by a scream from Sheila, who on Beaver's strict instructions had been sitting passive under the tangled rigging, not daring to move.

A rope had somehow wound itself round her ankle and she was being dragged up the mast upside down. I have never seen a woman being dragged upside down up a mast before, and I must say the spectacle was most interesting. In fact if it hadn't been for the others I would have seen if we could have got her to the top.

Eventually the mast swung upright, the base thumped into the socket and I rammed home the piece of metal which secured it.

'Hoist sail,' shouted Beaver.

This was easier said than done. All the ropes had tied themselves into obscure knots that would have taken hours to tie deliberately (why is it that left to its own devices a rope ties a knot much more complicated than anyone could invent?). I was just trying to unravel the jib halyard when Beaver called, 'Stand by to fend off.' We were drifting gently into a motorized wherry moored by the bank.

We struck the wherry a soft glancing blow. A red-faced man in a blue jersey appeared and created as much fuss as if we had rammed her at full speed, demanding why we came 'down here' barging all over the river and scraping people's paint. I notice that this type of person always makes his criticisms from a vessel fitted with a twenty-horsepower engine. I have never met one actually sailing. It is one thing to shout at people in yachts and wear a blue jersey and look professional and quite another to sail a yacht yourself. It all didn't quite measure up to the legendary comradeship of sailing, but then I find that idea rather exaggerated anyway. For every person who invites you over for drinks there's always someone who will shout, object to your presence, ask you to move or criticize the way your boat is lying. My experience is that a person's friendliness deteriorates as their boat gets bigger.

Unfortunately, we couldn't get away from the man, because in the confusion of raising the mast we appeared to have lost a vital rope and while we gently rocked alongside him he just stood there and shouted insults. In the end we couldn't stand it any longer. Harry waited until we were ready to sail, kicked off our bows, and thinking we were safe shouted a remark which translated into pure English was: 'Why do you not go away, oh Illegitimate One.'

How we all roared! 'That'll teach him,' chuckled Beaver

as we came about. 'The bloke's a raving lunatic.' The next moment our mirth was cut short. The wind died and we found ourselves drifting back helplessly towards the wherry.

The red-faced man was still there. 'Call me that foul name would you?' he bellowed. 'I'll give you language I will.'

Once more we gently struck the wherry. It was as if we had released a hidden spring in the man because he didn't stop insulting us for five minutes while all the time we feebly tacked to and fro, making no ground and receiving fresh abuse every time we came about. In the end we got clear and as we drew ahead Beaver had the last word.

'Do you mind repeating all that?' he called. 'I'm afraid I'm rather deaf.'

The incident cost us our lead over Arthur, who sneaked past on a freak catspaw of wind, but we caught him up round the bend and then followed a grim battle for the lead. Arthur sailed by the book, demanding his rights according to the rules of racing.

'Give way to me Beaver you old clot!' he shouted, 'don't you know Rule 38 forbids a windward vessel to curtail a luff?'

Beaver didn't, but he used to invent a few rules of his own ('Give way, Arthur, can't you see I'm fore-reaching') and when those failed he simply got out a boathook and pushed Arthur's stern round. Occasionally as we swung close together I could see into the cabin, where Joan was beating up eggs in a bowl.

These frolics passed the time pleasantly enough until we came to the riverside village of Stokesby, two miles downstream, and Beaver shouted to Arthur that we ought to stop for a drink.

Arthur agreed and started to manoeuvre *Quiet Dawn* to the bank. And then an astonishing thing happened. As he came alongside he passed close to a motor-cruiser going in the opposite direction and Dennis's cat, which had been mewing loudly in the bows, leaped on to the other boat.

It was all over in a moment and I was the only one who noticed. I shouted to the cruiser and to Arthur, but the cruiser was out of earshot and by the time Arthur and Dennis understood what I was saying he was past the bend and heading for Acle at six knots with the cat washing itself on the stern.

There was only one thing that could be done. Arthur swung *Quiet Dawn* round, and with the wind behind him headed forlornly upstream after the cruiser, Dennis in the bows shouting, 'You've got our cat on board, give us back our pussy.'

They, too, disappeared round the bend. The sun shone and all was silent except for the lapping of water and cries of 'Pussy, Pussy' in the distance. We went for a midday pint with great peace in our hearts.

Rolling Down to Burnham
(A sea shanty)

Oh, sitting in the yacht club
A-listening to the wind
I spied a pretty maiden
A-drinking it-and-gin.

    Chorus: With a rifo, rifo, stick it up the mast-oh,
            Away, away, look away.

Oh she did look so pretty
In her sweater chunky knit
That I upped me anchor straight away
And by her I did sit.

    Chorus: With a rifo, rifo, stick it, etc., etc.

Oh maiden, maiden, maiden,
When will you marry me?
Alas, I cannot,
Actually I'm engaged to a rather nice chap who
    works for an oil firm.

    Chorus: With a rifo, rifo, etc., etc.

Rolling Down to Burnham

Words by Michael Green
Music by Guy Eldridge

6

Lunch was slightly farcical. Sheila cooked some spaghetti and then had to leave it while she tried to drag us back from the pub and when we returned it had fused into the bottom of the saucepan (a fortune awaits the man who will invent non-glutinous spaghetti). We amused ourselves by scraping it off and smothering it in sauce, pepper and anything else that came to hand, and then *Quiet Dawn* came into view before we had finished and moored at the staithe. At first we couldn't see the cat and then Harry spotted it peering out of a cabin window with an expression which clearly indicated it was planning further mischief.

Dennis carried it over and told us what had happened. Apparently the cruiser skipper had gone only a few hundred yards when the cat jumped on to the back of his neck. The shock was so great that he drove the boat into the bank. The cat then defied all efforts to catch him and led the man and his wife in a chase all over the boat. When Dennis sailed by chanting 'Pussy, Pussy' they hailed him with gratitude and almost offered to pay him to take the animal away.

Of course we all made a great fuss of the cat, which thanked us by eating a tin of sardines and climbing up the rigging, where it refused to come down. Finally we had to lower the wretched mast again.

Beaver chafed at the delay and as soon as the cat was rescued we set sail. From Stokesby onwards the River Bure rolls pleasantly through low-lying pastures for about three miles until the Stracey Arms Hotel is reached. After that, as one nears the estuary at Yarmouth, the river becomes foul, muddy, evil and treacherous, a trap for unwary yachts with shoals, mudbanks and swirling currents. At low tide the navigable channel is reduced to a few feet in places.

The weather changed in sympathy as we sailed past Stracey Arms. Dark clouds obscured the sun and a chill breeze sprang up. It was against us, of course. The wind is always against you when sailing, unless for some reason you want it that way, in which case it veers round and blows from astern. Don't believe the old saying that the wind changes with the tide. It changes according to the person who is sailing. I've only got to step into a boat for it to change completely. If necessary it'll blow vertically if it knows I'm coming. Many's the time I've set off with the wind in my teeth, anticipating a nice easy run back, only to find it veers just as I turn the boat round to come back. I remember this happening when I was trying to make Emsworth, in Chichester Harbour, with the result that the tide turned when I was just 400 yards short of safety. We remained completely stationary for half an hour and then one of the crew gave a fearful cry and shouted, 'Land is springing up all round us.' It was, too. As the tide fell great stretches of land were actually marching towards the boat. Finally the land caught us up and we spent the night surrounded by a sea of mud.

Beaver hated this stretch of the Bure, or the Cruel Bure as he called it. He hated it as if it were alive, swearing that when the river greedily swirled at the muddy banks he could hear it chuckle at him, mocking his efforts.

His fears were justified. It wasn't long before the boat slid to a standstill as we tried to come about and we knew we were aground. Now getting off mud is one of those tests which distinguish the good Coarse Sailor from the bad one. The first thing to do is to use the quant pole, either to push back the way you've come or to get the head of the boat round. We tried this and it sank four feet into the mud. Then we stuck it into the bank but a piece of earth gave way and Harry fell forward with his hands on the bank and his feet on the boat, like a human bridge. So Beaver decided that to break the suction under the keel we should have to perform The Dance of Muddy Death. In this, everyone leaps up and down on the stern to rock the boat, while someone else pushes with the quant at the bows. The trouble is that while it's a terribly serious business to those involved, anyone looking on thinks you're drunk. People in passing boats were highly amused. They all came on deck and rocked with laughter, asked Beaver for the next dance, requested an eightsome reel and all sorts of alleged pleasantries.

'Look at the fat one!' screamed a plump matron in one cruiser.

'I'm looking at her, madam!' shrieked Beaver in retort, as he danced maniacally on the transom.

In fact The Dance of Muddy Death is not so effective as swinging the tiller to free the keel. So while Beaver swung it to and fro mightily, Harry and I adopted the last resort, jumped overboard in the mud and pushed the bows round. It worked and as *Merryweather II* swung free, we clambered aboard and crawled aft, leaving a foul trail of black slime all over the deck, as if a couple of huge slugs had crawled that way. Incidentally, you've got to be careful with this jumping overboard. I once bounded over the side when we went aground during our Dutch trip and found the water was only a foot deep. The bottom was shingle and I sprained my ankle. All this in the middle of a lake. I felt an absolute fool.

Going aground isn't always unpleasant, of course. In calm weather on a sandy bank in the Solent it's a positive pleasure and I've had many a nice picnic resting on the sea-bed and sunbathing and thinking this is better than a passage to Weymouth. An old friend assures me that when he went aground on Ryde Sands, Isle of Wight, somebody on shore, thinking they were in distress, dialled 999. The lifeboat crew turned out but when they saw where he was they actually walked over to the yacht. They had a pleasant chat and then strolled back again.

Things were a little miserable on board, what with mud all over the place, until we found *Quiet Dawn* aground further on. A cruiser cutting across had wrecked her tack and she'd plunged so far into the bank a cow had stuck its nose over the bows. As we passed it started to lick the deck and all its friends were galloping up to join it. We could see Dennis bellowing 'Get off, you filthy brutes' and trying to repel them with a quant pole while Joan huddled in the stern, attempting to look as if she was enjoying it all. I noticed her immaculate women's magazine-type sailing rig was already stained by mud, fat and tomato ketchup. As we turned the corner out of sight a loud moo announced that Dennis had scored a direct hit with the quant.

Beaver was anxious to beat Arthur to Yarmouth and started to go too near the bank on the end of his tacks, so two minutes later he went aground again. Arthur sailed past as we pushed the bows round with the quant and *Merryweather* went across on the other tack. 'Ready about,' said Beaver optimistically as we neared the bank and then we slid to a stop as if a hand had seized the keel. We were stuck again.

'Go on, get overboard,' said Beaver irritably, when all other methods had failed.

We sat there, glowering at him.

'Don't fool about,' bleated Beaver, 'the tide's falling. We've settled down three inches while you've been wasting time.'

'You'd better hurry up then, hadn't you?' said Harry.

'What me? Go over? You must be joking.'

We sat firm and Beaver began to get piteous, saying he really would go over but he'd caught malaria during the war and it might bring it on again. Eventually he descended to wheedling ('I'll buy you a double Scotch each at Yarmouth') and we knew we'd won. In the end we rather wished we hadn't because he made such a fuss about entering the water that we had to go over and help him back into the boat, where he lay panting on the deck. But after that he took care not to go aground again.

We overtook Arthur fast aground on a notorious shoal just by the Smith's Potato Crisp factory at Yarmouth. Arthur must love that shoal. At any rate he spends half an hour there every year. On one occasion he spent the night fast aground on the mud. To stop the boat heeling over as the tide ran out he swung the boom ashore and pinned it to the earth with a rond anchor, a real Coarse Sailing wheeze.

Another method of keeping the boat upright in a similar crisis is to plunge the quant pole into the mud as a prop. It is important not to let the boat heel over, because when the tide starts making she may stay fixed in the mud and start to fill. A year or two ago we passed a young couple fast aground and heard them say, 'Well, we may as well stay here the night.' They answered our warnings with pitying smiles (Beaver may have been a little rude, of course) but next day we saw them standing miserably on the bank with the boat half full of muddy water.

I wish sailing instruction books would devote more space to practical hints like those I have just outlined. There are whole passages on how to join two pieces of rope together (why bother? why not just buy a longer rope?); advice on keeping weed off the bottom; hints on the correct procedure when landing abroad; hosts of diagrams about picking up moorings and so forth; but nothing about what to do when stuck hopelessly on the mud by some dolt.

I suppose, of course, one could fly a flag of distress when aground, but nobody seems to pay attention to them. My friend on the Hamble has a lovely collection ranging from 'I Am Discharging Explosives' to 'You Should Stop, I Have Something Important to Communicate to You'.

Well, one fine Saturday we went aground in Southampton Water and having nothing better to do we flew international flag F, meaning 'I am disabled. Communicate with me.' Boats came and went. Some passed quiet near. Quite a few exchanged greetings. But nobody knew what the flag meant. Eventually we flew our ensign upside down as well and when that didn't work we flew flag O, meaning 'Man overboard', and still nobody bothered about us.

As a last resort we let off a miserable little flare which my friend had kept for thirteen years, waiting for the ultimate emergency, and all that happened was that the boat was filled with smoke and a man passing in a motor-boat said, 'A bit early for fireworks, isn't it?' Heaven knows what would have happened if we had really been in trouble.

By the way, don't wait for an emergency before reading the instructions on a flare. It may be too late then. Some years ago I crossed the Channel in an eleven-foot Vagabond dinghy unescorted with an old pal called Peter (I apologize if there is a hint of boasting about this) and to our horror we discovered halfway across, in pitch darkness, that we had forgotten the torch and were reduced to striking matches at oil tankers. When these ran out we seriously considered lighting a flare but the fool who designed it had made both ends the same, so without light there was no way of telling which way up it was and we could easily have fired it through the bottom of the boat. And the directions were in tiny print so all we could distinguish in the moonlight was part of a warning:

ON NO ACCOUNT MUST THIS FLARE BE – and we decided it was safer not to fire it.

Yarmouth, which we were now approaching, is the supreme test of Broads sailing. The tide swirls viciously past the yacht station, immediately beyond which are three low bridges waiting to catch your mast. To make matters worse a high jetty and some houses take away the wind, while opposite is a treacherous shoal.

It is a standing amusement for the locals to come down to the yacht station on a summer's evening and watch the boats coming alongside. They come, not to see the graceful shapes gliding in to the jetty, but to hear the howls of dismay and fear as the aforesaid graceful shapes are dashed against the railway bridge with a snapping of timber. They are rarely disappointed.

Sunday evening is the best time, for Yarmouth is like a bottleneck between the northern and southern sections of the Broads and then all the yachts crowd in, ready to start on the morning tide. This week Sunday's storms had delayed everyone by a day and Monday evening was the busy one. The jetty was crowded as we rounded the corner and the wind, which had hitherto been persistently against us, immediately began to blow towards the jetty in fitful gusts.

However, Beaver, whatever his faults, does at least have a healthy respect for Yarmouth. There are all sorts of theoretical things to do but the golden rule is to start coming alongside as soon as possible so that if anything goes wrong there's still time to take action before hitting the railway bridge. Beaver came about and ghosted back diagonally across the stream, with a slack mainsheet and the tide taking off most of our way, and as we neared the jetty dropped the peak to scandalize the sail, while Harry hopped on to a moored yacht and made us fast. Apart from the fact that our boom nearly killed a girl on the moored boat, all was quite peaceable. Somehow I don't

think this method would be approved by the Royal Yacht
Squadron but it worked. No doubt in theory we should
have temporarily moored on the other side of the river,
taken off sail and quanted across but the last time we tried
it we spent hours on the mud.

As soon as sail was down we climbed up on to the jetty
to join the ghouls watching the other yachts come in. I
wouldn't miss the sight for anything. It's my annual treat,
the thought of which sustains me through the long winter
months. The first boat to come down was a Bermudan-
rigged sloop with a honeymoon couple on board. At least I
didn't know for sure, but they must have been
honeymooners because every other word was 'Darling'.

As they came round the bend the husband said,
'Darling, would you go forward and get out the
mud-weight, darling?'

His bride walked to the bows and stood looking
helplessly.

'Where is it, darling?'

'In the forepeak, darling. Under the hatch, dearest.'

Under a four-knot tide they sped towards the first
bridge.

'Can you find the weight, darling? It's rather urgent,
sweetheart.'

'Yes, I'm looking, darling, but there's a lot of luggage on
top of it, dear.'

The husband looked apprehensively at the bridge.

'Oh, do hurry, darling. We shall hit the bridge.'

'I *am* hurrying, darling. You'll just have to slow the boat
down.'

'A pause. Then: 'Darling, for God's sake get out that
blasted mud-weight and stop mucking about.'

The woman looked up, burst into tears and cried: 'Oh,
get your own stupid mud-weight, darling. I'm sick of you
and sick of this boat and sick of this rotten holiday. I *hate*
it.'

The bridge was about ten yards away. With commendable presence of mind the husband swung the boat round and plunged into the mud on the right bank of the river. He then started a slanging match with his bride, in the course of which I learned a lot of interesting things about their respective family histories, including the fact that the bride wished she had married a bloke called Julian. It was so interesting all the watchers applauded.

A man who stopped his yacht by scraping alongside all the moored craft was next and he was followed by Arthur. Yarmouth is Arthur's *bête noir*. He's never yet got in without being the centre of an admiring crowd, and his fans were not disappointed this time.

With a great shout of 'Boyur' *Quiet Dawn* turned into wind in the middle of the river and started to drift sideways towards the railway bridge at an alarming rate. Dennis poked the quant pole into the water tentatively and could not touch bottom. The jib had been dropped and the boat wouldn't pay off. Joan had been given her post of danger by the boom crutches and she stood clutching them and staring wide-eyed at the fast-approaching bridge.

Advice was hurled at them from all sides, as always. Beaver bellowed for Arthur to hoist his jib and get some way on. A group of locals called out for him to drop his mud-weight while a beery-looking person told him to start his engine. Meanwhile Dennis was trying to restore steerage way by rowing with the quant pressed against the mast, looking rather like an ancient Phoenician oarsman. Arthur was pumping the tiller to bring the bows round and shouting at Joan to start paddling with the deck mop.

When it seemed they must hit the bridge the yacht-station attendant arrived, scenting trouble, and hurled them a long line. Nobody paid any attention to it. Dennis was still prodding the river as if he expected to

… landed on Arthur's head

find gold there, Arthur was shouting and gesticulating and Joan was holding the crutches with grim intensity.

'Tell the missy not to bother about them crutches and to take hold of the line,' shouted the waterman.

Joan reached out a tentative hand and missed it. The waterman hauled it in and threw again. This time it landed on Arthur's head and he clutched it gratefully. They were so near the bridge that Dennis was using the Broadsman's last resort – fending the boat off with the quant pole on the bridge girders. But you can't keep it up for more than a few minutes, your arm muscles become tired and you're doomed.

A group of ghouls heaved on the rope and drew Arthur to safety.

'Not bad,' muttered Beaver. 'Usually Arthur manages to sink someone.' As he spoke there was a splash and Joan fell overboard, still holding the crutches.

We fished her out from the deck of a motor-cruiser the other side of the railway bridge, where the tide carried her. A woman on the cruiser, a motherly, middle-aged Northerner, was appalled as we dragged the poor girl from the water like a sack of potatoes, having first salvaged the crutches.

'Ee, you poor lass,' she said. 'Why do you do it?'

'Oh, we don't mind,' squeaked Joan bravely, rubbing the diesel oil from her face. 'It's *fun* to us.'

A COARSE SIGNAL GUIDE

Signal	Conventional Meaning	Coarse Meaning
Towel waved across mainsail	Help! *or* Open the swing bridge	I am drying the towel
Lighted piece of rag waved violently	Aid me	My cigarette lighter does not work. We are out of Camping Gaz
Man jumping up and down tearing his hair	—	My ship is going to hit yours unless you get out of the way! *or* Damn the stupid bitch, she's forgotten to stow the beer again
Barrel of tar alight on deck	SOS	I have just lit a barrel of tar on deck
Tea-towel flown from backstay	—	We have just washed up
Ensign upside down	SOS	I had a terrible hangover this morning
Ensign flown at night	—	We forgot to take it down
Burgee jerking up and down rapidly	—	It's stuck again
Short blasts on foghorn	Keep out of my way. I am manoeuvring with difficulty	Fascinating things, these aerosol foghorns. I can play with them for hours
Pair of trousers hung over rail	—	I am on my honeymoon
Loud cry of distress	SOS	What a stupid place to leave a hot kettle
Copy of *Reed's Nautical Almanac* ablaze on deck	—	*Either* SOS *or* I cannot work out these damned azimuth tables

7

Next morning I blew the boat up.

Like so many of the world's great events it happened quite casually, almost in passing, as it were. I got up early to make tea, as we planned to go through the three bridges on the last of the ebb. It was not my turn, but late the previous evening the boat was found to be in peril of drifting away, thanks to the way I had tied up, and this was a penance. The time was just after six o'clock on a dull, drizzly morning, quite a contrast to the previous day. It had been a peaceful night as we were all too tired to bother about Harry's snoring, although Arthur disturbed us by tramping round the deck in the middle of the night warning us the tide fell nine feet, as if we didn't know.

I opened the lid of the cooking locker, turned on the gas, struck a match and was enveloped in a sheet of flame. Out of sheer self-preservation I instantly jumped overboard. I swear I *hissed* as I touched the water.

The tide carried me away and I was fifty yards downstream before I managed to grasp the stern of a motor-cruiser moored by the jetty. The occupants had a shock when a white, shrivelled and dripping hand was thrust through a port-hole as I clambered aboard. I heard a gasp from a bunk immediately underneath, but I was past caring.

When I walked back to the boat they were all looking over the side and debating as to whether I could still be alive. This callous attitude appalled me. You get to know your friends on a trip like this. Beaver was actually saying,

... I instantly jumped overboard

'He must have gone down like a stone, we'll have to call out the police frogmen,' when I placed my hand on his shoulder and said 'Beaver' in sepulchral tones. He turned and went quite pale. Apparently I was dripping wet and minus one eyebrow, which gave me a slightly quizzical appearance.,

Beaver, after recovering, accused me of leaving the Calor gas turned on at the main all night, which I considered most unfeeling of him, although it was quite true. His chief concern was whether the boat was damaged. Since the explosion had felt like a bomb going off I was surprised to find it wasn't, and this rather weakened my story that I had been blown through the air for fifty yards, surviving only because of an iron constitution.

I claimed a glass of brandy from Beaver's private stock, which he always referred to as 'the medicinal stores', and had breakfast on my bunk, while Arthur regaled me with some yarn about a barrage balloon exploding in the war and how everyone thought they were all right and then they all dropped dead three days later from delayed shock.

I couldn't rest long because we had to take down the mast and shoot the bridges. Everyone else was doing the same and there was a rare old cluster of boats going through. There were boats going backwards, boats going sideways, boats going forwards and boats just stationary on the mud.

The official method of going through the Yarmouth bridges is to drop the mud-weight over the bows and drift down backwards with the tide, controlling your speed by letting the mud-weight brush the bottom. It is an incredible business and I have never known anyone achieve it successfully. We always rely on a good quant for steerage way, but one needs to know the bottom well, because in some places the river is too deep to quant while a few feet further on you're liable to go aground. If the tide is running fast, we keep the mud-weight handy on the stern as a precaution. One year Arthur found himself going too fast and threw the weight overboard to check the boat. He then discovered he had forgotten to tie the weight to anything and it sank with a mocking gurgle, lost for ever.

The scene on the River Bure as the tide changes is the nearest thing to a marine hell that can be imagined, with the yachts creeping down the river surrounded by a seething mass of powered craft, and the inevitable refugee from the M1 trying to force his way through at ten knots, waving his arms and blowing his hooter. In the middle of it all we met a man broadside on across the stream, trying to park his cruiser like a car. On seeing us approach he optimistically held up a hand for us to stop. Since this was impossible we had the biggest laugh for years before ramming him amidships.

Quanting under these conditions is a nightmare but we somehow got through. After passing the third bridge both boats moored at the coal wharf (although how it got its name is a mystery, as they never seem to unload coal there). The only alternative is to moor at the dolphins provided for yachts, but it is no use doing this for the simple reason that they are built on shoal and you will certainly go aground if you moor on the first two at low water.

The coal wharf is an old stamping ground of ours. Often we have spent the night there after shooting the bridges at dusk. It was here Dennis walked straight off the jetty into the river on a pitch-black night and here that just after the war Beaver sprained his ankle tripping over a heap of old iron and lay calling for help for two hours before we found him.

The official tugman has his mooring near here, situated strategically at the junction of the Bure and the Yare, and makes a healthy living by pulling boats off the mud. He is a busy man, for the tides are strong and treacherous and the notorious Breydon Water, a four-mile stretch of mud partly covered in water, lies just ahead.

When we first sailed that area we always thought he was a sort of lifeboatman whose services were free. The first time we used him was when we went aground in a gale between Yarmouth and Stracey Arms, and Arthur's well-meaning efforts to tow us off broke our boom. Arthur sailed back to Yarmouth with the SOS and the tugman came out in his launch, with his little dog sitting in the bows (when it died a few years later we all felt we'd lost a friend). He towed us back to Yarmouth and on the way we debated how to reward him. In the end we decided he would be insulted if we offered him money and agreed to give him twenty cigarettes.

Harry leaned over the side when we tied up and said, 'Thanks very much old chap, that was most kind of you. Have a smoke on us.'

He took the cigarettes and handed over a bill for three pounds.

'And you be lucky,' he said, lighting a smoke. 'I charge extra for pulling 'em off Breydon.'

For years we tried to find out what his scale of charges was, but all he would say was that he charged 'a pound a tide, sometimes more, sometimes less'.

Basically, I think he charged according to whether he liked you or not. We nicknamed him Sinbad and as the years went by he got to know us so well that he often gave a secret tow for nothing, saying slyly, 'I won't let your pals know you had a lift.'

By some freak of nature the tide starts to make up the Yare an hour earlier than on the Bure, so as soon as the mast was raised and sail set we cast off, and with one gigantic heave from the quant pole to get under way we were at the junction of the two rivers. To the left lay

Yarmouth harbour and the sea, but hired boats are forbidden to enter the harbour and our course was to turn right, into the Yare, and sail inland.

The Yare is an important commercial river, in the old days a great wherry highway, and still much used by ocean vessels steaming up to Norwich. It is unusual in that its estuary is now inland and has become Breydon Water. There is a dredged channel in the middle about a hundred yards wide and desolate mud-flats beyond this, covered at high tide. It is typical of the stupid River Yare that having formed a nice estuary over the centuries it should go on piling up so much mud that the estuary became land-locked and now Breydon Water is separated from the sea by a strip of land and the river goes on to join the Bure and a new estuary outside Yarmouth. They built Yarmouth on the mud it piled up.

Beaver was chafing to get on, and we left *Quiet Dawn* behind. The first hazard on entering the Yare is a railway swing bridge, now fixed, but with nasty currents between the arches. The wind being fitful we drifted through the arch and were promptly seized by The Giant Hand. This is the name Dennis gave to a strange current just past the bridge which has a habit of seizing yachts without much way and casting them ashore. The wind dropped completely for a moment, then suddenly gusted from a totally different direction, and we were carried firmly to the mud at the edge of Breydon. Beaver cursed, shouted, swore at the wind and the crew, but without result. We grounded firmly on the desolate shore.

Fortunately, the tide was flooding, so Harry was about to quant us off the mud when we had a nasty shock. Sheila pointed out that the jib was covered in blood, strange red blotches spattered over the leeward side. It looked as if a gang of pirates had attacked the boat. What with the excitement of getting under way we'd not noticed.

'Come on, who's had the haemorrhage?' barked Beaver, who denied that the blood came from someone he'd flogged. We all examined ourselves carefully, and looked in each other's faces, and down our shirts, but we couldn't find anything wrong.

'Well, somebody's bleeding heavily,' said Beaver, 'and we ought to find out who it is. We can't go on in a boat slowly filling with blood.'

Just then Sheila gave an alarmed squeak.

'Look!' she cried dramatically, 'gory footprints!'

And there on the side-decking was the outline of a human foot in blood. Well, perhaps not a foot but a bit of a shoe anyway. 'I know that pattern,' said Sheila. 'It's Harry's new shoes!'

Harry sat down and took off his shoe. It was a cheap slip-on bought at a newsagent's. It was full of blood and he'd cut his foot quite badly. Something sharp had gone straight through the thin sole when he went ashore before sailing. Harry said he felt a sudden pain but was too rushed to stop (that's what happens when you get a skipper like Beaver). Then he'd bled over the jib as it lay on the deck while we poled our way through Yarmouth.

'The water's filthy, you know,' said Beaver. 'It's riddled with sewage and all sorts of muck. You ought to cauterize that wound. I can do it easily myself. You just heat a knife until it's red-hot and then you cut out the affected flesh.'

Harry agreed, provided Beaver first tested the knife on his own flesh, preferably near the groin, and there the matter rested.

Meanwhile Arthur sailed by, hailing us with some sarcastic remark about it not being a very nice place for a picnic. Arthur can be a little jarring at times. I could see Joan bending over the cooking locker, doubtless engaged in some expensive fricassee.

While Harry's wound was being washed, I pushed the bows off and we sailed away. Sinbad overtook us and exchanged greetings, saying he was going to make his third attempt to rescue a motor-cruiser which had gone aground on the highest tide for six months while taking a short cut outside the marker posts. Later we passed it, the occupants standing forlornly on deck while Sinbad described endless figures-of-eight round it. I must say it's rather bad luck when you go for a quiet inland cruising holiday and spend most of it marooned on a sea of mud but Beaver thought he recognized the boat as one which had caused our disaster at Acle Bridge and said he hadn't laughed so much since they cremated his former boss.

The wind freshened considerably as we came nearer to the centre of Breydon, and Beaver decided we should reef, as the boat was becoming difficult to handle.

Reefing under way, as described in the textbooks, is, of course, simplicity itself. The instructions usually run something like this:

'Now we must prepare for foul weather. Let us assume that the wind has risen to gale force and the boat is threatening to capsize. First, keep calm and do not run for harbour. Remember that drowning is not an unpleasant death whereas if you get on a lee shore you may be dashed to pieces against the rocks. Next take in a reef, or two if you feel like it. Head the boat into wind, nip smartly for'd and lower the jib, haul up the topping lift to take the weight off the sail, lower the gaff so that the cringle on the luff can be tied to the boom, roll up the leech between the first reef cringle and the clew, place it on top of the boom, tie the leech cringle to the boom, then roll up the sail carefully and tie in the reef points, and in a trice you are snugly reefed.'

Hmmm....
I think I could just manage all that in the middle of a

perfectly calm sea with no other craft in sight and all day to do it. My experience is that even when moored securely I have never reefed in under an hour and then I usually find I've tied something wrong somewhere and have to start all over again. The thought of drifting helplessly about Breydon Water out of control for two hours at nine-thirty in the morning doesn't bear thinking about.

Our experience this time bore out my impression. Beaver rounded up in the middle of the channel, and we took the jib down all right, and scandalized the mainsail. But by then we were drifting broadside on across the main channel, up which a large public pleasure steamer, named *Pride of the Broads*, was proceeding. I pointed this out to Beaver, who merely said we would have to be quick with the reefing, that was all. Well, I never was much good at knots and things, and by the time Harry and I had got that bit about the cringle done (I never really know what a cringle is, it sounds like a word meaning 'to slink away') *Pride of the Broads* was looming over us, loudspeakers playing music and its siren hooting.

Theoretically, of course, power craft give way to sail, but there is a little rhyme about

> 'Here lies the body of Harold Day
> Who insisted on his right of way.'

Beaver, however, shouted: 'Move over, you bloody great steam-kettle, can't you see I'm out of command? Give way, can't you?'

The *Pride of the Broads* replied by passing within two feet of us, so that Sheila squeaked with fright. The passengers peered down curiously from the deck above and one small boy spat on us (he missed, I'm glad to say). Beaver voided himself of two Anglo-Saxon words and was rewarded by a jeering toot.

As we were now drifting towards the mud, Harry and I untied our one miserable, knot and hoisted sail

'Move over …!'

again. I don't think Beaver noticed. He was still shaking his fist at the pleasure boat and swearing while a group of elderly people sitting in the stern nodded, smiled and waved at him.

Later, when we mentioned the incident to Arthur, he said we should have hoisted two black balls to show we were not under command. As if we were likely to find two black balls anywhere. In fact, I made up a rhyme:

> 'Here lies the body of Harold Halls
> Who forgot to hoist up two black balls.'

In passing I should like to say that hoisting black balls is not the only bizarre marine distress signal that is recommended in nautical almanacs. Others include lighting a barrel of tar on deck or firing a signal gun every minute. Naturally, every yacht carries a barrel of tar, two black balls and a gun. Why don't the handbooks give practical advice, like shouting, 'Mercy, save me, help, I'll pay anything, for God's sake ring the lifeboat!' etc.

We came to the end of Breydon Water at ten-thirty. Here there is another fork where the River Waveney runs into the Yare. It's a lonely, desolate spot – the loneliest in the world on a dark, drizzling night when one is trying to reach Yarmouth – but upstream lies some pleasant country on both rivers, although they are rather treacherous for a mile or two. Our route took us up the Yare to Reedham, where according to schedule we were due to lunch. The tide was flooding strongly so we had no trouble with the mud and we reached Reedham in splendid time, helped by a spanking breeze, mostly on the beam.

The river bends sharply to the right just before Reedham, where the New Cut joins it, and the approach to the village itself is guarded by a railway swing bridge. Like all Broads swing bridges this will open to let yachts and other tall craft through, but its normal position is closed. If a train is coming the signalman, provided he remembers, hangs out a board with a figure 5 or 10 to signify the number of minutes craft must wait. This figure can usually be multiplied by three to arrive at the correct solution.

The bridge was open as we came round the bend, and very pretty it looked in its white paint. It had an odd air of Victorian gracefulness. Beaver sprinted for the gap, if one can say that of a yacht. Through turning, however, the wind was against us and partly blanketed by the bridge, so we didn't approach it very swiftly. When we were a few yards away the signalman opened the window of his box, shouted a warning and started to close the bridge.

We had the choice of swinging round and retreating; or trying to tack through the narrowing gap before the bridge closed. Beaver, as might have been expected, decided he could beat the bridge and we watched in horror as a collision between it and our mast became inevitable. Beaver's mind works in an odd fashion. It didn't occur to him to give way; he decided the bridge ought to retreat, and stood up in the well making winding motions at the signalman, urging him to unwind the mechanism. Mercifully the bridge beat us to it, and its vast bulk swung past the mast, missing the forestay by perhaps two inches. As it did so the wind dropped away and we paid off into the piling posts beside the bridge where Harry jumped on to the posts and made us fast. I took off sail and we walked the boat back out of danger. I don't think Beaver noticed we had stopped. He was still making winding motions at the signal-box.

We waited a few minutes and a train passed over but the bridge didn't open. A further ten minutes and Arthur's mast appeared round the corner and Beaver began to get mad.

He cast off from the piling and sailed up and down in front of the bridge, shouting 'Bridge ahoy' as if it were a ship. We all felt the need for one of those little trumpets which Dutch boats use in similar circumstances. This produces a noise like a dying frog, and when the bridge controller hears the unmistakable sound he opens the bridge. I have known it to fail only once in Holland, and on that occasion we sailed up and down blowing for a quarter of an hour before a man in baggy trousers and clogs told us by signs that the canal was now closed. This was great news, because it meant we had travelled twenty miles to no purpose.

One reason why the Dutch bridges open so readily is the charming tradition in which the bridge operator hangs out a clog on a sort of fishing-line and you drop money into it as you pass. If you fail to drop in any money you will find all the other bridges mysteriously closed to your boat. The first time this happened none of us knew why the man was dangling this dirty old clog so ostentatiously, so we just smiled and waved and I thought he was offering the clog as a souvenir and actually grabbed it as we went past.

Like most Dutch canals, this one went through the centre of the village and we couldn't understand why two or three people ran along the quayside after us, waving their arms and shouting. It was most unlike the friendly Dutch. Finally we gathered we had done something wrong, and turned back. It all ended happily. We gave the man back his clog and his fee, and he informed us that we were flying the Dutch flag upside down, which solved another mystery, namely why so many people had shouted at us throughout the trip.

After a time the signalman came and looked out of his window and gazed down at us, smoking a contented pipe. He was obviously a person at peace with the world. Not so Beaver. When Arthur drew level and tacked to and fro his fury knew no bounds, especially when Arthur, who is a railway maniac, said he was rather pleased to have the chance of seeing a train as it went over the bridge.

'If you ask me,' Arthur called over the water, 'he's waiting for the eleven-eighteen up mail from Lowestoft to clear that there crossover near Somerleyton.'

'If you ask me,' retorted Beaver, 'he's a miserable old crossover himself, and I'm going to have words with him.'

I was on the helm at the time and Beaver ordered me to put *Merryweather* into the reeds by the bank. It took about five minutes to scramble across the field and up the railway embankment to where the signalman was watching us benignly.

He showed no emotion until Beaver bounded up the steps of his box, flung open the door, and demanded: 'What the hell is going on? Why won't you open the bridge?'

No one had ever done this before, not even the captains of ocean-going steamers which use the Yare, and he didn't quite grasp Beaver's meaning.

'You aren't allowed in 'ere,' he said, pointing the revolting stem of his pipe at Beaver. 'If you want the train you'll have to go down to the station.'

'I do not want any blasted train. I want you to open the bridge.'

'Ah, I can't do that, you see. Not without I get the all clear.'

'But we've been waiting a quarter of an hour.'

'So 'ave I, so 'ave I. I reckon 'e be a bit late.'

Beaver resorted to hurt dignity. 'Do I understand that we are expected to swan about in front of this bridge until this train arrives? How do I know it's not been cancelled or something?'

The signalman was quite patient, rather as if humouring a lunatic.

'Now, you look 'ere. If I opens that there bridge and that train comes along 'e's liable to fall in the river, isn't e' now? You wouldn't like that, would you? I'm sure you'd feel very much upset if you saw that train come tumbling down into twenty foot o' water. Think of them passengers.'

Beaver sighed. 'I am not asking you to commit manslaughter. Put one signal at danger to stop the train. Then open the bridge. Then shut the bridge. Then put the signal at green. It's easy.'

The signalman digested this for a moment and then shook his head.

'Ah, you see it isn't as easy as all that. Not by a long chalk.'

Beaver was about to make a rude retort when a bell tinkled.

'You're in luck,' said the signalman. ''E's coming.'

The train crossed the bridge as we slithered down the embankment. The bridge opened as we ploughed across the field. Arthur sailed triumphantly through. The bridge shut just as we jumped aboard and cast off.

For one moment I thought Beaver would have a stroke. Instead he contented himself with going straight below and compiling an immediate letter to British Railways beginning *'Dear Filth ...'*

We didn't see him again until Harry sailed us through ten minutes later and we tied up at Reedham village staithe.

Gentle Waterways, New Thrills

'First, the waters are smooth, and the tides and currents gentle. The reed-cushioned banks are never far away, and the water is mostly shallow – though deep enough for your boat. It is a safely-adventurous holiday, with new thrills which old hands regularly enjoy.'

Extract from a Broads holiday boat catalogue

8

The encounter with the signalman had wounded Beaver deeply. As soon as we had tied up he strode ashore, posted his letter of complaint to the railways, and then marched straight into the Nelson Inn where Harry, Sheila and I found him drinking beer with primeval noises, and muttering to himself.

The Nelson used to be a fine old pub. At least it may not have been everybody's idea of a pub but it was mine. It had a smoke-stained old ceiling, a picture of the ships of the British Navy in 1899 (and an incredible lot they were too) and a homely atmosphere. It was here that one year the girls shaved off Dennis's beard in the snug and later we condemned him to death and hauled him up the mast by fixing a jib halyard in his belt.

Now progress has overtaken the Nelson, like many other places. The brewers have rebuilt it and they've thrown 'The Ships of the British Navy' into the dustbin, along with a lot of other things. I often wonder why brewers spend so much money imposing an alien character on an old place when they could spend it better by improving the quality of the beer. I never can understand this mania to turn every country pub into a replica of a Great West Road gin-palace. A lot of them on the Broads have now installed juke-boxes, the thunderous beat of which rings monotonously over the water, ruining everyone's peace. For years we said we wouldn't drink in a pub with a juke-box only in the end we found that meant we weren't going to drink at all.

However, they still sell beer at the Nelson, which is the main thing I suppose, and the crew of *Quiet Dawn* soon joined us, with the exception of Joan, who was scouring Reedham for breadcrumbs for Duchess potatoes. When Sheila heard this she left and joined her for another branch meeting of the Women's Consolidated Trade Union. It's odd that women don't realize how few and precious are the drinking hours allowed to us. I can think of nothing more frustrating than waiting for women to join you in a pub. They tidy their hair, change their skirts, go back for their cigarettes and then change their whole outfit because the other girls are wearing slacks and all the time the golden minutes are ticking away. It's fatal to wait for them, unless you want to arrive just as the landlord calls last orders.

And to crown it all, after reducing an evening's drinking to a snatched pint, the women always bleat at closing-time, 'Oh, they're not shutting already, are they?'

Beaver was not exactly sociable. He was further upset by a tactless remark of Arthur, who said: 'I envy yew going in that there signal box. Do you think the signalman would show me round if I flashed my Enfield Model Railway Club badge?' He sat on a stool at the end of the bar, breathing heavily, chewing cigarettes and pouring gin into his beer. Arthur held forth at great length about the state of the railways round there and every time a train hooted leaped to the door. But it was pleasant enough, especially when the girls joined us in about half an hour, although I thought Joan showed signs of strain again when Dennis cross-examined her about the shrimp sauce.

At closing time Beaver broke a long silence by remarking suddenly: 'No lunch. I'm going to try to make Norwich.'

We glanced at one another. The combination of a few pints of bitter and several gins, together with Beaver's hurt pride, was likely to prove dangerous. Arthur shrugged and said:

'I reckon we'll have our shrimp sauce and Duchess potatoes first.'

After a brief mutiny by the crew of *Merryweather II* it was agreed to allow five minutes for a cold collation. We had scarcely sat down before Beaver arose and started to hoist sail by himself, muttering and chuntering away. He did not make a very good job of it because halfway through the gaff crashed to the deck, narrowly missing Harry's head. Finally he hoisted the sails in an appalling mess, vanished into the cabin and came back with a bottle of gin, helping himself liberally to the contents. Then he just sat glassy-eyed in the stern, grunting.

Beaver was tight.

Arthur and Dennis were having lemon-meringue pie as we sailed (Dennis was telling Joan it was a little overdone). We didn't make a very good start because Beaver steered us straight into the reeds on the other side of the river, but finally we lurched off in an unsteady fashion in the general direction of Norwich. Beaver's behaviour became more and more erratic, and the gin bottle emptier and emptier. At Reedham chain-ferry he cut across the bows of the ferry which stopped just before its chains would have carted us clean out of the water, and a mile further on he deliberately sailed into a herd of swans. Beaver hates swans, having been attacked by one as a child, and this gave him the idea of catching one, so for some time we sailed slowly back and forth while I held out an ingenious trap in the shape of a piece of bread on the end of a fork, and Harry held a noose of string on the end of a stick.

The idea was that the swan would swim up to take the bread, then I would carefully withdraw the bait so that the swan had no choice but to put its head in the noose. We never planned what to do with the swan when caught, but as we did not catch any the problem did not arise. I was rather pleased when the swans went away to attack a small boy in a rowing-boat because one of the first things I ever learned is that a swan can break a man's arm with its wing, since when I have imagined that they do nothing else.

Then we heard the steady thud-thudding of a steamer behind us. The Yare is a busy commercial route and ocean-going ships use it, sailing direct to Norwich from the Continent via Yarmouth. They have no room to manoeuvre in the narrow river and all a yacht can do is to get out of the way. This is not always easy, because while the steamers normally stick to the centre of the river they reserve the right to take the outside of a bend where the water is deeper or to go near either bank if it suits them. In other words, they are right whatever happens.

Over the years we've become used to them and don't usually have any trouble. The real danger only arises when there isn't any wind, or when the wind is astern and the channel narrow. I shall never forget a nightmare half-hour some years ago when there were five yachts stretched across the river with the wind astern, and a 500-ton Dutch coaster following twenty feet behind, so close that we could hear the captain swearing at us from the bridge, although I don't know what he thought we could do about it. He followed us all the way to Breydon Water where the channel widens out and we were able to make way for him.

When we first saw the ship it was about 300 yards away, appearing to sail along the flat fields, thanks to a curve in the river.

'Beaver,' said Harry. 'There's a steamer behind.'

Beaver glowered at it with bloodshot eyes and took another swig of gin.

'Just too bad, isn't it?' he replied.

We sailed on, ghosting down the centre of the river with a feeble wind on the beam, and no sound but the steamer's engines and Beaver's breathing. The sugar-beet

Beaver gibbered at it …

factory at Cantley was just ahead. That part of the river is protected by trees on one bank which cut down the wind, so we had little way, and the ship was catching up quickly. When it was about a hundred yards away it appeared to fill the whole river.

I coughed.

'Beaver,' I said, 'it's rather close. We could run into the bank nicely until it's past.'

Beaver looked at it again. 'It's a dirty foreign tramp,' he replied with a vile drunken belch. 'I don't give way to foreign vessels.' (Beaver had all his savings in Cunard shares.)

Harry showed signs of nervousness. He had a wife and children to think of. We could read the steamer's name quite plainly. It was French. We reached a bend and the wind now came from ahead. Beaver started to tack without a glance behind him.

When he made the first tack we all thought he had come to his senses and was clearing the steamer's path. The atmosphere lightened immediately. Harry started to light a cigarette, Sheila smiled and waved at the ship and Beaver took another drink of gin. But when we neared the bank he put the helm down and came about across the river. Next moment we were heading for a point three feet in front of the steamer's bows.

A wall of steel towered over us. Two startled French faces capped by berets peered over the ship's rail. Beaver stared ahead unseeing, his eyes glazed.

'Not giving way to power vessel,' he said thickly. 'British yacht never gives way to damn foreign tramp. Harry, tell the Frog to get out of my way.'

I believe that the *Manual of Seamanship* lays down that when a ship's master goes insane the officers may agree to relieve him of his command. The proper procedure is to say politely, 'Will you retire to your cabin, sir?'

Unfortunately there was no time for such niceties.

Harry seized the helm and tore it from Beaver's grasp. Beaver promptly snatched it back and they sawed it to and fro for a moment, until the gin bottle fell on to the deck and Beaver relinquished the tiller to make a grab for it.

The steamer missed us by what seemed a foot but may have been four or five. Beaver gibbered at it in an ecstasy of rage and finally flung the gin bottle at the stern. Harry steered the boat straight into the bank and we all just lay there with every emotion drained from us. Sheila was down below, praying, I believe. From over the water came a voice.

'Boyur,' it called, 'what are yew doing in them reeds?'

I never thought I should be glad to hear Arthur's voice. Normally, given a choice between listening to Arthur and standing next to a pneumatic drill, I would choose the drill every time. But on this occasion it sounded like the trumpets of Paradise, a call so clear and sweet that it pierced my very soul. I sat up and stared round like someone waking from deep sleep. *Quiet Dawn* was gently gliding over the river towards us. Joan peered excitedly over the side of the cockpit, holding a half-peeled potato.

'Did you see that big steamer?' she said. 'Wasn't it fun?'

'Pull into the bank,' I told Arthur weakly, ignoring Joan's well-chosen remark. 'We've had a spot of bother.'

Suddenly everyone was talking. The silence broke up into a torrent of conversation, as when a teacher leaves the classroom. Everybody babbled at the tops of their voices, saying what heroes they were and how they had never been so scared in all their lives, and the only silent person was old Beaver who sat glaring at the reeds. Then he stood up, swaying, and said: 'I don't feel well. Wanna lie down. Everything's going round and round. *Troppo multo* gin.'

He crawled into the cabin with a last slurred appeal, 'Wake me before Norwich.' He was asleep within ten seconds.

Arthur shook his head sagely when he heard the story,

which lost nothing in the telling, and he recalled a time when he and Beaver had a similar disagreement with an aircraft-carrier off Portsmouth.

'You'd have thought a naval vessel would have had the courtesy to give way,' he said, 'but she just kept on as if she owned the place. Mind you, I think Beaver was a little quixotic this time. He was morally right but practically wrong if you ask me.'

'He was drunk,' said Sheila acidly.

An unearthly moan from the cabin added point to her words.

We had a cup of tea and discussed what to do next. Norwich seemed a long way away and the trip would mean a lot of quanting because of heavily wooded banks. Arthur wanted to stop at Brundall so that he could visit the railway station there, which he said was the scene of an historic collision many years ago, but we overruled him and decided on Bramerton Woodsend, a quiet, pretty spot a mile or two beyond Brundall.

It was heavy going. The tide turned against us and we swung the quant pole until our arms ached. It was well after tea-time when we reached Bramerton and we were all so hot and tired that we stripped off for a swim, with the exception of Sheila, and Beaver, who remained unconscious.

That was a delightful swim. I don't think I have ever had a better. We plunged and gambolled around as merry as crickets. Sheila sat in the boat and threw bread to us and we all pretended to be ducks. Then Arthur did his imitation of a submarine, Harry tried to life-save Joan (and nearly drowned her) and Dennis chased a swan.

When the fun was at its height a small child rowed towards us inexpertly and sat staring.

'Hullo, sonny,' I said jovially, catching hold of his gunwale for a rest. 'Aren't you coming in for a swim?'

He didn't reply at once, but continued to brood. He then

said: 'I suppose people have got to go to the lavatory, haven't they?'

I didn't like this.

'Yes,' he went on. 'My dad won't let me swim in the river here. It's the sewage, he says.'

The sun went in. Somehow the water didn't seem so nice. Arthur was just diving under the surface and spouting like a whale. I shuddered.

The relentless child went on.

'It come down on the ebb tide from the dyke, my dad says. My dad says he wouldn't swim in this part of the river for all the beer in Norwich, my dad says.'

'Where's the sewer?'

The boy pointed to a bend in the river. 'Just round the corner. They open the gates when the tide's ebbing, *like what it is now*.'

I did not swim madly to the bank. I kept my head, paddling carefully in a bizarre fashion, holding the body perfectly upright with my face as far away from contact with the water as possible. As I dared not open my mouth, I didn't warn the others until I reached the bank.

Joan went berserk, poor girl, and shrieked, 'Oh no, it's all your fault, Dennis,' and swam to the bank as if pursued by a jet-propelled piece of effluent. Dennis went pale and tense and by some remarkable feat of muscular control actually launched himself out of the water from the waist upwards and moved vertically to the bank. Arthur feigned indifference and hooted with laughter, but he got to the bank first.

We were only just in time. The sewage dyke announced its presence five minutes later.

Looking at the chart we found the following legends marked near our mooring:

Sewage Works (Norwich Corporation)
Sewage Farm

Sewage Wharf
Sewage Dyke
Sewage Outlet
Old Sewer.

For good measure the bank was marked as lined with old wrecks and there was an inscription: 'Palaeolithic Implements found AD 1926.' What a place to put Palaeolithic implements.

But, as Arthur said, it was just as well we hadn't looked at the chart or it would have spoiled a lovely swim.

9

An ominous event happened when we returned from the pub at closing-time. I shone my torch in *Merryweather*'s well and a rat jumped up and ran ashore down the mooring-rope.

The effect on Arthur was alarming.

'Wild horses wouldn't drag me on board that boat of yours tomorrow,' he said. 'Even the rats are quitting. Mark my words, they *know*.'

Harry and I jeered at him, but rather hollowly. Of course, the rat didn't live on board, it was only a stray visitor, but the coincidence was rather disturbing.

Beaver was still in his bunk unconscious. Sheila had shaken him earlier and asked if he wanted any supper, but had been rewarded with a growl of such animal intensity she didn't ask him again. In view of that, and the rat, we decided to have coffee over in *Quiet Dawn*. As Dennis said, this would also give Joan a chance to *marinade* tomorrow's meat.

Then, while we were having coffee, the boat rocked violently, the cabin door opened and Beaver stood framed in the aperture, looking at the point of death.

'Is it a fact that we were nearly run down this afternoon?' he croaked. 'For heaven's sake tell me if it actually happened.'

We assured him it had happened.

'Oh, goodness me,' was his astonishing reply (the only time I think I have ever heard Beaver use the phrase). 'Oh dear, oh dear. I must have been boozed. I haven't been like that since the night the war finished in Cairo.'

We all felt quite warm to Beaver after that and assured him that the danger was much exaggerated and we were sure that even if the ship had hit us we were all good swimmers and would have survived.

Beaver's remark about VE Night in Cairo started a spate of reminiscence. We all knew one another's stories, of course, and waited politely for each to finish before dashing in with our own. The formula on these occasions is to say, as the laughter for the previous story dies down, 'I don't know whether I ever told you about the time I was stationed in North Wales ...' and everyone else, who has heard the story at least twenty times before, politely mutters, 'No, no,' and then the speaker launches into a tissue of lies based on some long-forgotten original incident.

Hearing these stories every year, it was interesting to see how they grew under intense competition from everyone.

When we first went sailing, Arthur used to tell stories in which he drove a ration truck. But as the war receded more and more into the past his truck got nearer and nearer the front-line and finally changed itself into an armoured reconnaissance vehicle. However, by this time Dennis's depot ship was sinking destroyers and Harry belonged to the only anti-aircraft unit that actually fought in front of the infantry. It was obvious *I* was the only person not exaggerating.

Arthur's trump card was his wound. He had injured his hand when he caught it in the door of a lorry outside a canteen in Farnborough, and it still bore a tiny scar. Now he carefully worked the conversation round to it, massaging his wrist and muttering 'Funny how my hand still hurts after all these years' before seizing his chance and leaping into some huge lie.

I must say Arthur excelled himself that night. Smoke

filled the cabin and we blearily blinked at him as he droned on and on, defying the enemy, cheating his officers and swindling the sergeants. Finally he told the story we had heard a dozen times before about how an Egyptian tailor sewed different flashes on each shoulder of his tunic and he was arrested by a Military Policeman on suspicion of being a spy. Only this year Arthur embellished the story by claiming he was waiting to be shot by a firing-squad when the mistake was discovered.

'They don't shoot you through the heart, you know,' said Arthur. 'They aim all over you. Every man aims at a different place. I was right scared, I can tell you.'

'Pity they didn't go through with it,' muttered Harry wearily as Arthur thundered on.

Luckily Arthur paused for breath for a moment and Dennis rushed in with his own story of how he drank too much at a wedding in 1954 and drove the car through the front garden fence. When his mother protested he said, 'I'm sorry, I haven't been like this since I was in Rome in 1944.'

'There you are,' said his mother triumphantly, 'it's becoming a habit with you.'

After that we went to bed tired but happy, apart from a slight whiff of sewage from the river.

It was about 2 am when I was awakened by a dreadful groaning. I switched on the cabin light and saw Beaver tossing and turning from side to side. I asked him what was the matter and he replied, 'Piles,' in a hollow voice.

Harry and Sheila were awake now and Sheila asked if there was anything that could be done. At first Beaver suggested a bullet through his brain but then recalled having some suppositories in his suitcase.

Sheila, who was in the forepeak, searched the suitcase and couldn't find any trace of the healing suppositories, but confessed perhaps that was because she didn't know what they looked like. Harry said he knew, so he searched the case, and he drew a blank as well. By this time I was contemptuous of their failure, so I had a look. True, I didn't know what a suppository looked like, in fact I didn't even know what it was, but I was sure if there was anything medical in that case I'd find it. Well, I turned it inside out and uncovered a fearful mess of stuff inside: dirty socks, old underwear, a compass, a pocket chess set and a flask of brandy, but nothing that could have been described as a suppository.

Of course I was looking for something like those strange straps and pads that hang in shabby surgical shops up the Charing Cross Road. I asked Beaver what they really looked like and he refused to discuss them or the method of treatment while Sheila was present. He made an effort to look for them himself, but the discomfort of crawling into the forepeak was too much and he gave up.

Sleep was impossible while Beaver kept complaining, so Harry got out the medicinal stores and poured him out half a tumbler of brandy, into which he crushed two aspirins, and then added some hot water.

Beaver's first reaction to this was to become talkative, and recall past occasions on which this illness, a family curse equal to that upon the ancient Scottish clans, had laid him low. But by the time he had drunk the whole glass his voice slurred and in the middle of some rambling reminiscence he fell asleep.

We all slept.

In the morning Beaver was no better and stayed in his bunk. A council of war was held and we decided to carry on with the schedule in the hope he would recover. Norwich was now out of the question, so the day's target was set as Beccles, a tough run but well worth it, for the Waveney, on which Beccles lies, is one of the pleasantest rivers on the Broads.

The day was sunny, warm and calm, and I hummed to myself while cleaning my teeth. Joan was cooking omelettes on the next boat and I heard Dennis reject his with the comment, 'No, thanks, my shoes don't want soling and heeling today.' I wondered how long Joan would stand it.

There was hardly a breath of wind as both boats quanted together back down the river, the sails flapping idly. Every so often a faint puff came, invariably from a different direction each time, and after a time we ignored these false alarms and slogged away in shifts of twenty minutes each.

Beaver recovered sufficiently to take an interest in what was going on, and having viewed the situation through a port-hole demanded that we make bigger efforts to overtake Arthur, who had crept ahead.

We stepped up the quanting rate just for the fun of it and Arthur, who can't resist a challenge, promptly accepted. Within a few minutes a demoniac struggle was going on. I've seen this sort of thing happen before, usually between Beaver and another boat. The race goes on until someone collapses or the wind springs up.

This time Dennis tried to steal a march by towing *Quiet Dawn*. As soon as we were clear of the trees he hopped ashore with a long line which Arthur always orders from the boatyard for such emergencies and trudged along the bank. This was fine until he came to an inaccessible section and had to relinquish the rope. Arthur drifted on while Dennis tried to find a way through the trees. He vanished from sight and then there was a long-drawn-out shout. When Dennis finally appeared it was obvious he had fallen into a nasty bog.

We were just past Brundall, both boats drifting down the centre of the river, when we heard the familiar thump of a steamer behind. I put the tiller over to bring us near the bank and Dennis did the same on *Quiet Dawn*. Nothing happened. We had no steerage way and continued to drift helplessly along, blocking the centre of the river.

Harry seized the quant pole and started poking but we

knew it would be useless. No quant pole has ever reached the bottom of the Yare at that point.

I said earlier that getting off mud was the true test of the Coarse Sailor. I should have added another supreme test – the ability to make way without wind or quant.

'Paddle,' I screamed, as the steamer, hooting continually, bore down on us.

Like good Coarse Sailors they knew what to do. Sheila dived into the cooking locker, produced the frying pan and started paddling on the port side. Harry did the same with the cabin mop on the starboard. I seized the tiller and started pumping it to and fro like mad. Over on *Quiet Dawn* there came a splash as Dennis jumped overboard with the bow rope and started to swim towards the bank, pulling the boat's head round, while Arthur copied me and pumped the tiller.

The astonishing thing is that all these methods actually work. We reckon tiller-sawing and paddling will produce a speed of half a knot, which is usually enough to get out of the way at least. And so it proved. We drifted slowly into the trees as the steamer passed and gave us a final hoot. As it did so there came a terrible noise from below.

Harry tore open the cabin door to find Beaver gibbering on his bunk with his hands over his eyes. Apparently he had been asleep, and woke up to see the side of the steamer blocking out the light of the port-hole as it went past. After the previous day's experience, the sight had been too much for him.

The wind improved as the morning wore on and we reached Reedham by lunch. On the way we made a small detour up the dyke to Rockland Broad so we could say we had at least seen a Broad. Thanks to the various crises, it didn't look as if we were going to have time for anything more than battering up and down the rivers. We had to stop temporarily at Reedham because Dennis's cat fell overboard while chasing a butterfly, but we resisted the temptation to visit the Nelson as we had a long way to go.

After the cat was rescued Sheila had the bright idea of closeting it with Beaver, thinking it would cheer him up, rather as they tried to please King David in his old age by presenting him with maidens. The idea was sound in theory, but it did not work. After two minutes there was a scuffling and a squawking below and Beaver called out that he was being clawed to death by a wild animal which had got into his cabin.

Sheila went below and found that the cat had its claws entangled in Beaver's beard, so neither of them could move but just lay staring at each other. It was such an unusual sight that we all came in to have a look, which did not please Beaver. Harry said, 'We'll just have to cut off your beard, Beaver,' which produced a roar of protest and the counter-suggestion we cut off the cat's legs.

Sheila solved things by stroking Pussy until he relaxed his claws and he was transferred back to *Quiet Dawn* by means of a rugby pass.

The swing bridge gave us no trouble this time ('They must have got my letter,' shouted Beaver from the cabin) and we passed through with no more difficulty than might be expected in trying to sail through a narrow gap where the wind is cut off. Then, instead of retracing our route along the Yare to Breydon Water, we swung off up the New Cut. This must be the oldest new cut in existence. It was built about 150 years ago to provide a shorter route for wherries sailing to Norwich from Beccles and Lowestoft, and now serves the same purpose for pleasure craft. It used to be spanned by a charming little lifting bridge, which we nicknamed the Van Gogh Bridge. If you didn't want the bother of taking down the mast you had to tell the signalman by the railway line, and a few minutes later a porter would cycle along and open the bridge, charging a toll of two shillings. Now the bridge is replaced by a modern road bridge, which has been brilliantly designed so that it is just six inches too low for a yacht's mast, although Beaver claims some boats can scrape under at low tide and with a heavy crew and if they don't mind losing the burgee. A typical Beaver statement.

The New Cut joins the Waveney near Haddiscoe railway swing bridge. The wind had dropped here and we drifted out of the cut helped by a poke or two with the quant. The tide was running strongly upstream towards the bridge, which was open. It was lovely to be on the Waveney and Sheila filled the kettle for tea. Harry stopped quanting and lit a cigarette.

The signalman leaned out of his box and shouted that he was going to close the bridge.*

I put the helm over to come about and nothing happened. We had no steerage way and continued to drift down on to the bridge. Harry jumped up, knocking the kettle over, and seized the quant pole. As usual when you need it in a hurry, it had entangled itself in the shrouds. They are malevolent things, quant poles. When you don't need them, of course, they obtrude themselves, getting in the way on every possible occasion, but when they're wanted in a hurry they go on strike and tie themselves up in the nearest rope. In the end Harry freed the pole and plunged it into the water.

It would not touch bottom.

'Don't close the bridge,' I shouted to the signalman.

'Train's on the way,' he replied, and added as an afterthought: 'And the trains round here don't float.'

The bridge began to close. Harry threw the quant pole on the deck and began to paddle with the cabin mop. I waggled the tiller. But it was too late.

As the bridge swung across I had a moment of delirious exultation. Surely this was the sort of thing old Jem Green

---

* Since this was written the railway line has been closed and Haddiscoe Bridge is always open, thank heavens.

would have revelled in? After all, I was at the helm, the man in command.

I see the tiny ketch being pounded to pieces in full view of the little fishing village, while the villagers fire off maroons in all directions and sing 'Abide With Me' on the quayside.

I cup my hands to my mouth, the rain streaming from my oilskins.

'Lower the boat, lads. Look lively.'

'Us caaaan't, Cap'n Jem. 'Er be stuck, loike.'

I stride from the tiny bridge to the boat falls, and with one blow of my ham-sized fist free the jammed pulley, using the other hand to pull back some craven-hearted coward trying to get in the boat first.

'There you are, lads. Jump in quick now.'

The frail boat is lowered, perilously full.

'Jump, Cap'n. Jump in before it's too late.'

'Not I, lads. There's no room. Save yourselves. I order yew.'

'God bless yew, Cap'n. Yew be a right 'un, yew be. Push off, lads.'

I raise my arm in salutation. The village choir change to 'Those in Peril on the Sea'. The boat gives a lurch. With a growl of defiance, I fling myself into the churning sea and strike for the shore, not even bothering to take off my oilskins.

A sinister clanking cut short my reverie. The bridge was closing. Jem Green faded and a pallid city-dweller took his place.

'Every man and woman for himself,' I squeaked ungrammatically. Harry pushed a reluctant Sheila over, jumped himself and I followed. We looked rather silly floundering in the water looking up at the bridge.

At this moment I realized Beaver was asleep on his bunk below.

Old Jem Green

The bridge caught the mast as it swung closed and the boat heeled to an alarming angle. There was a sharp crack and the mast fell down.

What followed is rather confused in my mind. Certainly the most noise came from the boat, where it appeared a young bull had been let loose. There were blastings and swearings and cursings as we swam towards our battered hulk to reboard it. Finally Beaver stuck his head out of the cabin door, stared at the tangled wreckage about him, and simply said, 'Upon my pile.'

He didn't even offer us a hand as Harry and I clambered aboard (Sheila had wisely swum to the bank), but continued to gaze about him, calling upon his illness every so often.

While we were making for the bank as best we could the bridge opened, Arthur sailed through without any trouble at all and started the conversation by asking if we noticed the unusual locomotive that had just passed over. Harry said no, but he had noticed the unusual yacht that had just passed under, the one without a mast and with a bearded lunatic gibbering in the cabin doorway.

'Come to think of it, yew have lost your mast, haven't yew?' pronounced Arthur, after a long look at the wreckage. 'What are you going to do, like?'

'Mike is going to ring the boatyard,' put in Beaver firmly from the cabin, where he had retired.

'Oh no, I'm not,' I retorted. 'I'm not going to face that bloke Loudwater. You know him best. You've had this sort of accident before.'

'That's exactly why I don't want to speak to him,' said Beaver with some logic. 'Besides, you were at the helm. It's your responsibility.'

'Let Arthur do it,' I suggested. 'As it's not his boat, Loudwater can't complain.'

Arthur shrank. 'No fear, I wouldn't ring old Loudwater for all the tea in China.'

I went to find a phone.

This was not easy and when I did find a call-box the bell rang a long time without answer. That was a bad sign. It meant someone would be coming a long way to reply and would be in a bad temper. I could imagine Loudwater himself being awoken from a siesta by the riverside and painfully limping to the telephone. However, just as I was about to put down the receiver there was an answer.

'Hello,' said a soft Norfolk voice. 'Loudwater's yard.'

'Ah.' I ran out of anything to say and prevaricated. 'Is that Mr Loudwater's yard?'

'Yes. Loudwater's yard here.'

'Er ... is Mr Loudwater there?'

'No.'

'Thank God – I mean how distressing.... You see, this is *Merryweather II* here.... We've had a spot of bother.... Ha, ha, ha, nothing much really, ha, ha, ha....'

'*Merryweather II*, eh? You're the people that had that trouble at Potter, didn't you? Boat with a bearded skipper, chap as knows Mr Loudwater?'

'Yes, that's us. We – ha, ha – well, the fact of the matter is ... ha, ha ... we've lost our mast.'

There was a long silence. Then the man said:

'Dear, dear, dear, dear, dear. Oh, dearie me, I don't know what Mr Loudwater's going to say about that. I'll have to cycle up to his house and tell him, you know.'

'Do, by all means,' I said magnanimously. After all, we couldn't object to Loudwater knowing we had wrecked his boat. 'But what are you going to do about it?'

The man wasn't sure. We were to quant to St Olave's Bridge and they'd try to send a lorry round with a new mast. Perhaps tomorrow morning, perhaps never. It depended on how Mr Loudwater felt.

'By the way,' he added, 'Mr Loudwater's very upset about that business at Potter. You know that woman who had hysterics hasn't left her bunk yet? Just lies there moaning and groaning. You've let us in for something you have and no mistake.'

I was rather pleased when that conversation finished.

As might have been expected, there was no praise for my heroic deed when I returned to the boats. Beaver said I should have insisted on speaking to Loudwater personally and given him a piece of my mind about his short quant poles which wouldn't touch bottom in a crisis and his rotten masts which fell down at a touch. Dennis said I should have demanded a new mast within the hour or else threatened to stop our cheque.

Poor old *Merryweather* was an awful mess. We tidied her up as best we could and quanted the mile or so St Olave's, downstream, where we laid the broken mast on the bank and prepared everything as far as possible to make the repair easier.

Beaver retired to the cabin again and we all sat round on *Quiet Dawn*, waiting for the pub to open, and talking despondently. Joan didn't take part in the conversation as she was under strict orders from Dennis to concoct *sole bonne femme*, and this isn't easy when you have to cook on your knees. I wondered when Joan's rebellion would come. While I was wondering she gave a great shriek and hurled the fish into the river. I must say I hadn't thought she would react as violently as all that, and then I saw the reason. A rat was sitting on the bank, staring at the boat.

'Mark my words,' said Arthur solemnly, 'them rats *know*. Fate hasn't finished with us yet.'

Of course, it's all exaggerated …

'… the quant would not hold bottom so far out and we watched our boat drift broadside on into a lump of darkness pierced only by the glimmering hole of the low side arch. Across that we stuck fast, our bowsprit shaking like a reed with the strain. An attempt to make her lie more comfortably, or haply to get her stern through the arch by hauling ashore on a line from her head, resulted in such an ominous crashing of planks in the dark, as made us prefer to sit all night supperless, watching for dawn and the ebb tide.

'We floated off in the cold grey morning, and a gale sprang up against us that rendered the first reach unsailable.... Five or six times we hopelessly set ourselves to quant up that reach without breakfast and as often we were drifted down; at a certain point we either had to go ashore or the quant lost bottom.'

Extract from an article 'A Cruise on the Norfolk Broads' by R A M Stevenson, MA, in *Outdoor Games and Recreations*, published by The Religious Tract Society in 1892. The author is describing an attempt to shoot Somerleyton Swing Bridge in the dark. Things don't seem to have changed much since then.

10

That night the cat died.

It must have been heart failure after the day's events. Arthur found he had passed away as he made his usual stroll around the moorings at dawn, and immediately woke us all up blubbering with grief and saying the rats *knew*. Pussy was buried before breakfast after a pathetic ceremony in which the little cadaver was gently lowered in a shallow grave in some nearby marshes. A wreath made of reeds was laid on the top and the whole surmounted by a picture postcard of Potter Heigham bearing the words POOR PUSSY.

I like to think someone would do as much for me some time.

Not unnaturally, this event cast a gloom over the proceedings. We were a sorry crowd as we sat drinking our third cup of coffee and waiting for Loudwater's lorry. However, in the middle of our misery Beaver emerged from the cabin whooping with joy and clutching a small packet.

'I've found them!' he cried. 'I've found them!'

'Found what?' asked Harry.

'My suppositories. They were tucked in the end of my shoe. You don't know what this means to me.'

It must have been a long time since anyone at St Olave's had bawled the word 'suppository' at the top of his voice and several startled faces were turned in our direction, especially as Beaver was so overjoyed that he danced round all the moored boats, waving his packet triumphantly and shouting the good news to all and sundry. I'm sure one or two people thought he had won the Pools. Anyway, they congratulated him and he shook hands and showed them his packet and seemed surprised when their faces dropped and they backed away in alarm.

Beaver now vanished for five minutes.

He returned wreathed in smiles and exuding bonhomie all round. Those little things must be wonderful.

Loudwater's lorry arrived at nine-thirty with a new mast sticking out fore and aft. I retired to a safe distance in case Loudwater himself was there and wanted to cross-examine the helmsman, but he wasn't, although one of the men said he had taken to his bed after hearing of the accident.

It took about two hours to step a new mast and a very fine job they did of it. Norfolk boatyard craftsmen are superb, and take a great pride in their work, although they sometimes adopt a cynical air. Their idea of a 'rough old job' is something with a Chippendale finish, even an emergency repair. But I never knew one of them ever admit to a piece of work being anything but 'an old botch-up'.

No sooner was everything ready than Beaver, now his old self, demanded an instant start for Beccles. None of us was very keen because it would mean an almost impossible journey the next day, which was the last full day of the trip. But Beaver produced a load of optimistic figures about how easy it would be with the tide if we got up at dawn and we gave in. Besides, we really like Beccles. It's our favourite spot.

We sailed without any startling incident for about an hour in a fair breeze, but about two o'clock signs of disturbance were noticed on board *Quiet Dawn*. Voices were raised in the well, Joan's being prominent. Beaver sailed as close as possible so we could spy on them and we heard Joan saying: 'No, I won't cook you any lunch. I spend all my time kneeling on this wretched floor with Dennis's stinking feet treading all over me while you two have all the fun. You can cook the lunch and I'll sail the boat.'

Dennis and Arthur regarded her rather as the beadle must have regarded Oliver Twist when he asked for more.

'Sail the boat?' exclaimed Dennis. 'You must be joking, girl. Now get on and put that spaghetti on to boil. We're hungry.'

'Ah,' added Arthur. 'I haven't eaten for two hours.'

'No,' said Joan firmly. 'You put on your own rotten spaghetti and I hope it chokes you.'

Dennis tried wheedling. 'But, Joan,' he said, 'you don't know how to sail the boat.'

'Then you teach me. And I must say that from what I've seen of Mike I could sail as well as him' (that was most unfair).

The argument went on for about ten minutes, during which their sailing suffered and we drew ahead. However, we were delayed by a gentleman in what appeared to be a floating saloon bar who drove us into the reeds and *Quiet Dawn* hove into view round the bend. At first I thought she was on fire. A dense cloud of white smoke covered the well and a voice was calling out oaths and curses. I then realized the smoke was steam coming from a pot of boiling water in the cooking locker. Arthur was on the deck tending the pot by abusing it, its contents and its mother in a loud voice. He had apparently burnt himself and had one hand stuck in his jacket like Napoleon.

Joan was steering.

The wind was on the beam so she couldn't really go wrong, and Dennis was holding the sheets and directing her, every so often putting his hand over his eyes as she headed for the bank or another boat.

Beaver slowed our progress so we could enjoy the

Joan was steering

scene. I'm glad he did so, for I saw a sight that will live long in the memory, even longer than my recollection of the vicar blowing up his church hall while working the effects for an amateur performance of *Journey's End*. As *Quiet Dawn* rounded the bend and the wind came from astern, Joan allowed her to gybe and the boom clouted Arthur across the cockpit as he was about to drain the water from the spaghetti.

The boiling water must have gone over Dennis's feet because he rose like a helicopter and hopped about the well. Arthur raised an anguished hand smothered in hot spaghetti and began wringing his hands to get rid of the stuff (a good deal of it flew across Joan's face, giving her an interesting appearance).

Quiet Dawn was approaching a boat moored by the bank in which four Sea Scouts were enjoying a meal. Joan put the helm over to clear them and put it the wrong way. As often happens with a novice, when she found she was pushing instead of pulling she merely pushed all the harder. *Quiet Dawn* turned neatly and headed for the Sea Scouts' boat with naval accuracy.

'Joan,' shouted Harry. 'Pull it the other way.'

Joan turned and gave him a ghastly, hysterical smile, before pushing the helm even further. Dennis and Arthur were still wrapped up in their injuries and didn't even notice what was happening.

It was an odd sort of collision. *Quiet Dawn's* bowsprit went neatly through a port-hole on the Scouts' boat, almost as if it had been aimed there. There was a crunch, a tinkle, a chorus of surprised voices, and there she was swinging gently with her bowsprit in the Scouts' cabin.

At least the collision shut up Dennis and Arthur for a moment. Joan sat in the stern staring at her handiwork and then burst into tears.

The Scouts were very decent about it (one suspects they had done the same thing themselves in the past). They also insisted on applying first-aid to Dennis, Arthur and Joan, as well as one of their own crew who had been sleeping on a bunk when *Quiet Dawn*'s bowsprit entered the cabin like a swordfish coming aboard.

They were very keen and rather overdid the first-aid. By the time they had finished Dennis looked like one of those cartoons of people with gout. Joan was treated as a serious case of hysteria and the first Scout to approach her clouted her violently on the face and poured a bowl of water over her.

However, in the end it was all sorted out and we parted on good terms. After that Arthur and Dennis sailed *Quiet Dawn* into Beccles.

On the way there was a distant rumble of thunder. Beaver reacted in an alarming manner and immediately handed over the helm.

'It usually hits the helmsman when it strikes,' he said encouragingly. 'Especially when you've got a metal tiller, like us.'

He then told a dreadful yarn about sailing with a man who had a steel plate in his skull as a result of a war wound, and who was struck by lightning while crossing Poole Harbour.

'It was terrible,' said Beaver. 'He glowed like an electric light bulb and then slumped to the deck. When he came out of hospital he had to wear a rubber hat for the rest of his life.'

A likely tale.

We reached Beccles about seven. It had been a hard, thirsty day, with a fair amount of quanting on the final stretch, and as soon as sail was down and stowed on both boats all the men started to march off for a quick one before supper.

Sheila and Joan had been muttering together by the staithe and Sheila stopped us by calling out, 'Hey, where do you lot think you're going?'

'To the boozer,' Harry replied patiently, as if explaining something to a dense child.

'You're not,' said Sheila. 'You're cooking the supper. Joan and I are going to the boozer.'

'I believe the women are revolting,' said Harry.

'I know they are, but they can't help it,' said Dennis smartly. This did not help matters. There was a tightening of female lips and a tossing of curly heads.

'Don't be silly,' was Beaver's contribution. He found conversation with women difficult and the situation was beyond him.

'This is mutiny,' said Arthur. 'Mutiny is an ugly word.'

'Joan and I are merely being sensible for the first time,' said Sheila firmly. 'Are you men going to cook supper or not?'

'But I cooked the lunch,' said Dennis in a pained voice.

The girls' reply was to roar with laughter.

Surprisingly it was Beaver who let us down.

'All right,' he told the girls. 'We'll cook supper. And we'll show you just how it should be done. Only you've got to go and have a drink. Is that fair?'

The girls agreed it was, and off they went with much giggling.

To make the preparation easier it was decided to have a joint meal between the boats. There was quite a lot of cooking experience among us, gained painfully in bed-sitters in Birmingham and Earls Court, and we were by no means helpless as long as all the food came out of tins. It was decided to have tinned soup, followed by tinned stew and tinned peas and carrots, and rounded off with tinned fruit and cream. We could not go wrong and as an extra treat Arthur undertook to make some dehydrated mashed potato.

There seemed no point in putting on the stew until the girls were in sight, as it would be hot enough by the time the soup course was over, so we broached the medicinal stores and smoked and told jokes and swapped yarns. Then as we saw the girls coming across the grass to the staithe we all bustled to our respective jobs.

Harry was chief cook: my job was opening cans. I'm a great one for can-opening, I've had so much practice in my life. I just flew at every can in sight and opened it wildly, while Harry poured the contents into the saucepan, giving it a professional stir every so often.

First there were three tins of stew and then the tins of vegetables and then the fruit and cream. I knelt on the deck opening away and passing them up like a conveyor belt. At last I finished the final can and as I did so Harry gave a little gasp. He was peering into the saucepan with an odd expression.

'Mike,' he said in a strained voice. 'I've poured the pineapples and mandarins into the stew.'

We dined off soup, mashed potatoes and cheese.

When the girls complained I pointed out that during the war I had eaten an exactly similar meal which the orderly officer had described as 'a nutritious and satisfying dinner'.

Afterwards we adjourned to the Cambridge public house, as we do every year we visit Beccles. Old Harry, the landlord, always lets us use the back room with the harmonium on which we play dismal dirges and where we can sing without distressing the other customers too much. Harry told us of a crew he'd just seen painfully tacking to and fro across the river with the wind *behind* them.

'What are you doing, tacking with the wind behind you?' shouted Harry.

'It's all right,' came the reply. 'We know this stretch well. *We had to tack up it last year.*'

In some mysterious way, via the Broads grapevine, Harry had heard of our unpleasantness at Potter Heigham, and about our mast. Another man in the bar said Loudwater was breathing fire and slaughter but we comforted ourselves that perhaps he was exaggerating.

The evening ended with Arthur playing 'Abide with Me' on the harmonium (an elderly man in the public bar was observed to cry during this) and we weaved a rather unsteady way back to the boats. We had stopped in the square to render the sentry's song from *Iolanthe* when a window was flung up violently after the first verse and I cringed in anticipation.

'That was very nice,' a man called out. 'Give us another.'

I *do* like Beccles.

Back in the boats medicinal stores were broached and we continued singing in *Quiet Dawn*. It was one o'clock before we went to bed, which would give us four hours' sleep before a five o'clock start in the morning for our last complete day.

I was having a final cigarette in the well when a voice called out 'Fire!' and before I knew what was happening someone directed a hosepipe at me from the bank. Having thoroughly soaked the whole boat they retreated with a cry of 'Boyur'.

All hands were immediately summoned to arms and half an hour later we crept along the bank to Arthur's boat with the intention of casting it adrift. But as Beaver, Harry and myself were creeping along the bank on all fours a policeman cycled up, shone his torch at us and asked what we were doing.

A question like that is rather embarrassing. I suppose one could reply 'I am crawling along the bank on all fours' or you could say 'It's all right officer, I always walk like this.' But any Englishman confronted by the Law is immediately struck into incoherence. Not that it matters what you say. By the time they've taken it all down a word at a time and read it out in court in one of those special droning voices they keep for statements by the accused, the defendant always sounds like a hardened criminal

('You've-got-me-bang-to-rights-guv'nor. It-is-these-black-outs-I-keep-getting.')

Fortunately, the constable accepted our explanation that we were playing a merry jape and we crawled off to cast *Quiet Dawn* adrift, when suddenly a jet of water poured over us. It was Arthur, lying in ambush by the water-tap. He kept hosing us down and roaring with laughter until he saw a good deal of the water was going over a policeman standing behind us, and then the water dribbled away and a ghastly silence rent the air.

It took the rest of the brandy and two cups of coffee to pacify the policeman. I think the brandy did the trick. He was almost friendly by the time he'd finished it sitting in the cabin dripping water all over the place. There aren't many places like Beccles, more's the pity.

At three o'clock we retired to sleep.

SOME PEARLS FROM THE MUDBANKS

Small drops of water falling on the face are usually a sign of rain.

Once a packet of detergent spills into the bilge you may as well give up the trip unless you like sleeping in a cloud of foam.

If the boat smells pump out the bilge.
If it continues to smell a change of crew may be desirable.

Watch the seagulls – if they are walking instead of floating it is time to come about.

Beware of the man who says: 'This boat is unsinkable. I defy you to capsize her.'

If there is a foul tide and no wind, and darkness falls before you can make port, *don't worry*. I'm afraid I can't think of anything that will help you, but it is absolutely essential not to worry.

Never sew cork into the seat of your trousers unless you are prepared to stand for the whole voyage.

It is no use telling the truth. Yachtsmen don't know what it means.

An elderly yachtsman is one who reefs too soon.

The one certain cure for seasickness is to take up golf.

11

We arose at five o'clock. It was dull and overcast. There was no wind. Everyone had a hangover and felt tired after two hours' sleep. Then after quanting out of the dyke we discovered the tide was still against us. Beaver had got us up for nothing.

Both crews were out of sorts and irritable. But then, that's usually how I feel when sailing. I can't think how the idea got about that boating is healthy. The average sailor spends the time sitting down, either in a yacht's well, on a bunk or in a bar, usually in an unhealthy hunched-up position and frequently in the wet. No wonder we all put on weight in the summer and need a good, healthy dose of city life to take it off.

True, yachting does occasionally involve frenzied outbursts of activity, such as when the outboard motor won't start or when you have to row or quant. But these merely cause harm through unexpected strain. Many a rupture begins on a yacht. The ruddy tan of the elderly yachtsman is more likely to be due to blood-pressure than health. Sailing's bad for the stomach too. I don't mean merely sea-sickness, but the harm caused by those vast fry-ups, those feasts of tinned food, and corned beef sandwiches and crisps and endless cans of tinned beer and midnight noshes and gin at three o'clock in the afternoon and brandy at three o'clock in the morning. And food prepared with hands covered in harbour slime, and bread that's been trodden on the cabin floor. Not to mention mooring near a bad smell.

Feeling low, we began to bicker among ourselves and even the placid Harry became testy. That's another danger of yachting. It changes the personality. Ordinary men turn into raving Gauleiters, charming girls become shrieking harridans, lifelong friends become sworn enemies. I've even known partners in a boat end a cruise by drawing a chalk line across the middle to indicate their own half after a quarrel.

The whole company turned irritably on Beaver, who gave some feeble explanation about contrary winds delaying the tide. Quanting against the tide is a mug's game and we all felt exhausted when the wind started to rise about seven o'clock.

The trip was uneventful except that near the entrance to Oulton Dyke we saw a youth standing in a field, and he shouted to us, 'Have you seen my father?'

'No,' shouted Beaver irritably, 'have you seen mine?'

Undeterred by the heavy sarcasm the young man shouted that his parents had dropped him there in a dinghy at six o'clock the previous evening for some fishing and had never returned. He'd spent the night under a hedge.

Since no deaths had been reported we couldn't enlighten the lad. He was still asking passing boats for news of his father when we passed out of hearing. We didn't think any more of the matter until half an hour later we saw a cruiser speeding towards us and a man shouted, 'Have you seen my son?'

I'm afraid it was just too much for us. Both boats burst into gales of laughter, in the middle of which Harry could be heard solemnly intoning, 'And when did you last see your father?' Between giggles we managed to inform the man where his son was but we were laughing too much to find out exactly what had happened. One of life's little mysteries.

At St Olave's we moored to take down the mast before

going under the bridge and Arthur was dismayed to see a policeman approaching him.

After examining the boat in silence the policeman said, 'Are you the hirer of *Quiet Dawn* here?'

'I have no statement to make about last night,' said Arthur firmly. 'The officer assured me he would say nothing more and I took his word. In any case it was all a ghastly mistake.' He added with a flash of inspiration: 'I was nearly wounded at Dunkirk, you know.'

The policeman looked puzzled.

'I don't know what happened last night,' he said, 'and I don't want to know. But I do want to know if you're the boat that threw your cat overboard yesterday.'

Arthur paled. 'Well, I did have a cat like …'

'According to what I'm told, you tied a brick to his neck and threw him overboard.'

Arthur almost blubbered at the injustice of this.

'I never tied a brick to him. Anyway, Dennis buried him. I wouldn't have hurt a hair of his lovely little head. He died of fright after the other boat hit the bridge. I put him in the marshes.'

'I know that. You didn't bury him very deep, did you? He floated out at high tide. As if he were accusing you, like.'

It took Arthur and Dennis half an hour to convince the policeman that they were the victims of the village gossip.

The policeman then said he was enquiring about a report concerning a boat careering around in front of steamers on the Yare. Arthur said he knew nothing about that while Dennis ran in front of Beaver's boat and held up a blanket to hide the name. I think the policeman thought he was insane.

We were glad to leave St Olave's. Breydon looked leaden and sullen as we approached via the treacherous mouth of the Waveney. It's not easy tacking up that stretch on the ebb tide when one mistake in the narrow channel can put you aground for eight hours, or even eight days if the tide's a freak. Beaver recalled seeing a boat go aground in a gale at the top of the highest tide of the decade. It literally vanished into the reeds, which closed behind it, and when the tide went down it was high and dry with cows grazing around.

Near the Yarmouth end of Breydon we went aground inside the marker posts (everybody who goes aground swears they were inside the posts, but this happens to be true). As the wind was blowing us further on to the mud, and the billowing of the sails made quanting difficult that side, I volunteered to go over and give a push. Unfortunately, this can be dangerous on Breydon. The mud wasn't firm and I sank deeply. For one awful moment I didn't think I was going to stop and I'd be like something out of an old movie, crying out, 'The treasure is hidden in … gurgle … gurgle' as I sank.

Still, I was able to give the bows an almighty shove to get the head of the boat round, the wind caught the jib and she suddenly paid off and started sailing away on the other tack. As she surged round I was left floundering on my face. By the time I was upright and shouting, *Merryweather II* was moving into deep water, Beaver and Harry busy with the sheets.

I really must have looked an idiot standing up to my waist in the middle of Breydon Water calling for help. It was also very uncomfortable. The tide was running so swiftly I could feel the mud moving. To comfort myself I pulled a cigarette from the chest of my waterproof and lit it.

A motor-cruiser approached with two young men and two scantily clad girls staring in surprise at the sight of someone standing in the water smoking a cigarette.

'It's all right,' I called. 'The marker buoy has sunk and the harbour commissioners have asked me to stay here for a few hours until it's repaired. They've given me a bell in case of fog. Please keep to starboard, if you don't mind.'

... standing up to my waist in the middle of Breydon Water

Another cruiser switched course to examine me. It was driven by a bald-headed man in braces who nearly ran me down. His wife peered at me curiously.

'Aren't you cold, luv?' she said at length.

'God bless, you, no, madam,' I said. 'You get used to it. The only human buoy between here and the Nore, I be. They allus calls out old Jem Green when they be in trouble. Beware of the shoal, if you please.'

'I wouldn't like your job,' said the woman. 'Alf, do you hear what the gent says?'

Alf replied by jerking his boat into full throttle and nearly running me down. I retaliated by pointing an accusing finger at him as he passed, and I like to think he was afraid of being reported.

My absence was noticed on board *Merryweather II* after they had gone a hundred yards on the tack, but for various reasons they took a long time to come up for the rescue and when they did so Beaver refused to approach nearer than six feet in case he ran aground again.

I stepped a pace forward to walk as close as possible to him and vanished beneath the waves. I had forgotten that the dredged channel on Breydon is twenty feet deep. My cigarettes were a pulpy mess by the time Harry hauled me aboard.

The entrance to the Bure, from which we had emerged four days before, was the usual maelstrom. Arthur had been unable to make the turn into the Bure, as the wind was cut off by buildings and jetties, and was now trying to claw his way back from the direction of Yarmouth harbour.

Merryweather nearly suffered the same fate, drifting sideways with the tide as the wind failed, but Harry rescued us with some sterling quant-pole work, and we made the coal wharf. There was an hour to wait before slack water which we occupied in getting down the mast and making tea. Arthur spent the hour sawing to and fro in the cross-currents between the Yare and Bure and calling down vengeance on them both. He had to wait until the ebb slackened before he could come in.

We quanted under the bridges and tied up at the yacht station to raise the masts. We had been on the go since dawn and felt dirty, sticky, tired and unshaven. Once more the dreaded unseen force tugged at our ankles and against our will we found ourselves marching towards the White Swan. It was nearly closing time but our thirsts were big and we managed to slake them. Then we returned to the boats with the intention of getting as far as we could on the rest of the tide.

'Start in half an hour,' shouted Beaver. 'I'm just going to lie down for a few minutes.'

'No time to waste,' agreed Arthur. 'I'll just have ten minutes horizontal while Joan goes shopping.'

Within two minutes everyone was lying down in the cabins, except Joan, who had fallen asleep in the well over her shopping list. The afternoon sun blazed down.

The wash from some maniac driving by at top speed awoke me. I had a headache and a taste in my mouth and when I looked at my watch I couldn't focus for a minute. Then I saw that it was four o'clock.

My first inclination was to turn over and go to sleep again until I remembered we had to return the boats next day. I sat up in alarm and shook Harry who muttered 'Go and tell your Mother' and turned his back. It took several minutes of shouting and shaking to arouse him and Beaver and then I went over and broke the news on *Quiet Dawn*.

The boats were due back at the boatyard at 10 am next day, and the yard was nineteen miles away – probably five hours' sailing. The best we could hope to do was go as far upstream as we could with the last of the tide. We set sail at once, moving slowly and clumsily like men in a trance, yawning and rubbing our eyes.

The stretch of the Bure upstream from Yarmouth is equally unpleasant whichever way one is travelling. True, the tide was with us at first, but the wind was against us and it faded away as the sun sank lower. Then the tide turned and the two boats crawled painfully upstream, stopping occasionally to go aground. Progress was only possible by having someone standing in the bows with the quant to bring the boat's head round at the end of each tack, another old Broads trick. By nightfall we had reached a desolate, deserted stretch somewhere short of the Stracey Arms Hotel.

Hired boats are not supposed to sail after dark on the Broads, although we had done it before in emergencies. We carried on a further half-hour and then moored by a section of bank which sounding with the quant pole revealed to be slightly less treacherous than the rest. Even then we were careful to moor well away, lashing the two boats fore and aft and using the mud-weights as anchors.

Usually we have a special feast on the last night, using up all the food that's left. A typical menu might contain soup, followed by eggs, bacon and tinned carrots, cold lambs' tongues in jelly, salted peanuts and a pound of cheese per person. But when the girls came to prepare they found we had no water, no bread and no tinned food with the exception of seven tins of sardines. True, the food locker was full of packets, but they were all useless things like gravy powder, corn flakes and custard.

And worst of all we were down to the last match. The box was full of dead ones ('Woe to him, God rot his socks, Who puts dead matches back in the box.') So we had to keep the Calor gas burning if we needed a smoke. I wish I'd supervised the stores instead of leaving it to Harry and Sheila, because the first item on my sailing shopping list is always ten thousand matches and fifty toilet rolls. It's too late to remember matches when it's low tide, you're on the mud for eight hours, and there's no way of lighting the stove for a cup of tea. And as for the toilet rolls ... all I can say is that an Admiralty chart is a poor substitute.

It was one of the most indigestible meals I have ever had in my life, consisting of sardines, boiled eggs and jam, without any bread and nothing to drink except brandy. It's surprising how you miss bread when you haven't got it. A great aching void appears in the middle of you, a sort of hole which only bread will appease. At first we tried to compensate by drinking large quantities of brandy, until finally we felt on fire and yearned for water to quench the flames.

In fact, as Jem Green might have written in his log:

Five hours out from Yarmouth. No water. No bread. The crew have gathered in a circle and are staring at me.

Dennis suffered most, being an habitual gourmet. In the end he said he couldn't stand it any longer, he simply had to have some coffee at least and he decided to go ashore and reconnoitre for water from a farmhouse. As he blamed Joan for not laying in fresh supplies at Yarmouth, he insisted she came with him to carry a jug and a saucepan.

They were gone a long time. We sat about, groaning with indigestion and trying not to drink the brandy, and telling one another how much we yearned for a nice cup of coffee. Meanwhile Arthur entertained us with a tale about how, during a winter trip, he answered a call of nature by going ashore, so as not to disturb everyone. Unfortunately, as he was crouching in a field, a frozen reed pierced his fundamental orifice, causing deep distress. 'Until you've had a frozen reed up your arse, you don't know what pain means,' he declared.

After an hour we become anxious and peered through the gloom for them, but there was no sign and it must have been nearly midnight when they were heard crashing through the reeds.

There was something odd about them. Dennis was giggling stupidly as he came aboard and Joan was flashing her eyes from side to side and lowering the lids modestly. I am not a suspicious man but I would have laid ten to one that a little of the old how's-your-father had been going on out in the fields.

Beaver, however, had a mind for only one thing.

'Where's the water?' he said. 'Let's have it quickly.'

Dennis's face expressed surprise.

'Water?' he said foolishly. 'Water? We – you see there wasn't – that is we never got any.'

A shout of anger rent the night. I thought Arthur was going to die from sheer thirst and disappointment. Beaver was the first to recover and he demanded in a menacing fashion, 'Why isn't there any water, Dennis?'

Dennis looked like a schoolboy caught doing something wrong and actually scraped one shoe up and down his trouser leg. It was Joan who answered.

'Dennis and I are going to be married,' she said dramatically.

A further howl tore the night air, this time of surprise and disbelief. It was hardly flattering.

Harry sat back on his haunches and rocked with laughter. Arthur said 'Boyur' five times in succession and Beaver simply stared. Sheila went up and kissed them both, thus showing she had a much nicer nature than the rest of us.

Beaver summed up his feelings thus: 'This is the end. I've seen everything on this trip. Pregnant women on board, cats in the rigging, masts coming down, and now a marriage. Would anyone like to complete things by announcing that they are a reincarnation of the Venerable Bede?'

We toasted the happy pair in neat brandy, forgave them for the water and settled down to sleep. Sleep.... Macbeth was comatose compared with us that night. Tormented by a raging thirst, racked by stomach pains, we tossed and turned until dawn, when out of utter misery we arose and quanted along the misty river. At Stracey Arms we dashed ashore for water and relieved the worst of our worries. After that there was enough breeze to hoist sail and we made good progress to Acle Bridge.

It was ten o'clock when Acle was reached, the hour when the boat should have been delivered. Thurne Mouth was passed at eleven-thirty, and it was nearly one before *Merryweather II* and *Quiet Dawn* were quanted into Loudwater's dyke.

We had cleaned and tidied the boats under way, so we simply unloaded our luggage in an untidy heap and made a beeline for the pub. I went to the bar to order and became aware of a tall, cadaverous person sitting morosely on a stool, staring into space. He pushed his glass across the counter with a shaking hand and quavered, 'Another port, Bill.'

'Certainly, Mr Loudwater,' said the barman.

I clapped the wretched boat-owner on the back.

'Cheer up, Mr Loudwater,' I cried, with well-meant joviality. 'We've just brought *Merryweather* back safe and sound. Have a drink with us.'

Loudwater started violently.

'You from *Merryweather*?' he asked, looking at me as if I was about to knife him.

'Yes.'

'Thank 'ee. I'll have a triple port in this glass and, Bill, this gent's paying.'

I persuaded him to join us, which he did with much shaking of his head.

'You won't be using my yard next year, will you?' he begged. 'It'll ruin me. I'm giving up yachts and building only motor-cruisers with sides two inches thick. Just promise you'll never come back, will you?'

Harry bought him another triple port and he mellowed

a little, regretting the decline of sail and recounting his early days on the Broads. We left him drooling over his third glass and bemoaning the fine craft he had known.

Joan and Dennis were in the pub garden as we stepped outside to go home. They were giggling and holding hands, as people will do in their circumstances.

Joan turned and waved madly at us.

'I say,' she screamed, 'wasn't it *fun*?'